How to Teach with a Hangover

Related titles

Teacher's Survival Guide 2nd Edition – Angela Thody, Barbara Gray, Derek Bowden
The Ultimate Teachers' Handbook – Hazel Bennett
Sue Cowley's Teaching Clinic – Sue Cowley
Guerilla Guide to Teaching – Sue Cowley
How to Survive your First Year in Teaching – Sue Cowley
Primary Teacher's Handbook – Lyn Overall, Margaret Sangster
Secondary Teacher's Handbook – Lyn Overall, Margaret Sangster
Everything you Need to Survive Teaching – Ranting Teacher

How to Teach with a Hangover

A Practical Guide to Overcoming
Classroom Crises

Fred Sedgwick

continuum
LONDON • NEW YORK

Continuum International Publishing Group

The Tower Building
11 York Road
London SE1 7NX

80 Maiden Lane
Suite 704 New York
NY 10038

www.continuumbooks.com

First published 2005
Reprinted 2005 (twice)

British Library Cataloguing-in-Publication Data
A catalogue record for this book is available from the British Library.

ISBN 0–8264–8597–9 (paperback)

Typeset by RefineCatch Limited, Bungay, Suffolk
Printed and bound in Great Britain by
Ashford Colour Press Ltd, Gosport, Hampshire

For my son Daniel with all my love

Contents

Acknowledgements

This book is an attempt to learn for myself, in the first place, about problems that beset the teaching profession, and also, in the second, to help other enthusiastic teachers to learn about these problems. Some are timeless. Others are rooted in the final 20 years of the last century and the early years of the present one. Of course, my book is selective. It would be: I have been a teacher in various capacities – student, classroom teacher, deputy head, headteacher, freelance poet in schools and colleges, university tutor – since 1965, so the book represents my experiences.

I am grateful for the help of friends and colleagues, especially Duncan Allan, Dorothy and David Hampson, Stephanie Lacey, Peter and Mary Moore and Daniel Sedgwick. All crudities that remain are mine.

Introduction

'In a perfect world, everybody would want to be a teacher. Other jobs, like the President's, would be done by those who weren't good enough to teach.' I saw this notice, or something like it, in the staffroom of a United States Air Force school in Norfolk. The school was the best-equipped I'd ever seen, the furniture comfortable, the library containing (I remember) sets of several encyclopaedias, the shelves of books as up-to-date as the *Guardian*'s children's book pages. There were computers everywhere, at a time when many a large British primary would have been lucky to boast more than a dozen. The place gleamed.

These were the days of the Clinton presidency. It has a stronger resonance as I write at the beginning of Bush's second term, with the clearer understanding it has given us of the United States and its Armageddon-threatening mixture of fundamentalist Christianity and war-like politics. I remember saying to a teacher, 'This is the richest school I've ever seen in the state sector'. I got a wry look. 'That is the power of the Defence Department.'

That notice looks arrogant as I type it now. What about all the other professions? They seem important too. I thank God for doctors and nurses who have made me better, and priests who have listened to me in my worst times. I thank God for Pip, who has made my cars driveable for the last 20 years (and for Robin, who did that before I met Pip, and who died of cancer) and for Kevin, who builds up the bits of my house that are falling down, and who paints things that I can't bear, or can't be bothered, to paint, and repairs things I haven't a clue about. I thank God for journalists who have made the first minutes of my waking day bearable (when I have had time to read them – usually that time is spent in my car outside schools before starting work with strangers).

I thank God, most of all, for artists: poets, novelists, dancers, musicians and composers who have helped me to enjoy and endure, who have helped me (by the same two tokens) in the search for the truth. Or, more likely, *a* truth: each poem, as Keats wrote, in a letter to his publisher, quoted in Vengler 1998, is 'a regular stepping of the Imagination towards a truth'. And that is true of all art. It is also true of education, but more of that later. As each poem is (as Robert Frost says somewhere) a 'temporary stay against confusion', so is each moment of learning, each insight into ourselves and our relationship to the rest of the world.

As I list these professions, I notice two things. First, I have excluded, without thinking about it, any rich people. I think of A. S. Neil, quoted by Edwin Morgan (1990) saying that 'If I create a millionaire ... / I've failed!' That is, I have failed if I teach someone whose main aim is the accumulation of money, who has forgotten, or never known, or, worse, who has wilfully ignored St Paul's injunction: 'the love of money is the root of all evil.' I've failed if I've helped to create those who successive governments laud as the 'entrepreneurs', whose eyes glint with silver rather than the light of common affection; who look (in Blake's formulation) at the sun, and see a guinea rather the Heavenly Host singing.

These governments lie. They tell us that life for all of us will be more prosperous because wealthy men's riches (I use the sexist noun advisedly) 'trickle down' to the rest of us. The verb 'trickle' is interesting: the wealth doesn't flood down, or even flow. It comes to the common people in a mean little dribble. And, in any case, it doesn't trickle, or dribble either. It stays where it was meant to stay, with the rich and powerful.

While I enjoy the produce of the best brewers, they are not on my list. I don't mean the big ones, of course, 'the men, the men, the very bad men, who water the worker's beer', but the local ones with English yeoman names in English counties, like Adnams of Suffolk, Shepherd

3

How to Teach with a Hangover

Neame of Kent and Brakspears of Hampshire. But even these solid men are not on my list.

There was a more optimistic surprise than the first. The professionals on my list – doctors, nurses, priests, mechanics, builders, journalists and artists – are not as different from teachers as one might think. They have all taught me. Doctors and nurses cannot make me better without teaching me something about my body. I may, if I choose to listen to them, learn from them. The best priests I've known (though I have mostly been in awe of them, or even fear) have helped me to understand the nature of the human relationship with God.

The mechanics, like my hairdressers, possess potential as teachers, but have usually told me less than I want to know. I feel that I could make more of a teacher of them. The man behind the chair with the clippers merely wants to tell me about his holiday in Tenerife: the flight, the movie, the bus drive to the resort, the hotel swimming pool, each meal, and the digestive consequences of it, and why he is thinking of going to Lanzarote next year.

But I'd like to know about the way a carburettor, or an air cooler, is fitted, or the way a hairdresser is trained, or the way he designs this style or that, this mullet or that crew cut. I love the way Kevin the builder, who definitely is a teacher, explains what has to be done before he does it. To climb to a higher educational level for a moment, think of a midwife explaining the process of birth to a mother- and father-to-be.

Introduction

And artists can't lift a brush, carve a lump of stone or wood, dance, tap a keyboard, choreograph a movement, sing a note or build a cathedral – can't do any of these things without being teachers. I was in Canterbury at a Solemn Eucharist for All Souls' Day with my son. This is the day when Christians traditionally remember and pray for the dead. I learned through all the senses that cold Wednesday evening. The incense, clanged quietly into a cloud in the air of the chancel from the swaying censer, taught me through the sense of smell. The Book of Common Prayer taught me, in its traditional Protestant way, through words. The pictures all around me, of Christ being born, being baptized, of his miracles and teaching, of his dying on the cross and his rising from the dead, taught me in the Catholic way, through images. The music, the early English columns, the taste of the wafer on my tongue, the altar rail, all these taught me in their own ways. I can learn through sight and sound, and taste, and feel, and smell, and in the cathedral, art was one of my teachers.

Professionals, whether working with medicine, with cars, with bricks, with words, with all the elements of art or with the elements of the Eucharist, are teachers. They all offer, on widely different levels, the chance to pay attention, and to learn, and to understand. While that placard in the USAF school may seem to be arrogant, it is excusable in the face of the common denigration of teachers as those who 'can't do'. In any case, it summed up something that I've always sensed in my long career as a teacher. It's the highest calling, and it's a component in the jobs of all the best people.

But what about those of us who teach a more specific way, those of us who see an adolescent in the high street, and say, oh, I taught him? Those of us with various qualifications, ranging from the plain CertEds of teachers qualifying in the 1960s, through the BEds of later years, to the MAs and PhDs I see flaunted now.

Teachers can do – have to do – so many things for which they have no training. And they do these things every working day. There's instant first aid, ranging from applying plasters to dealing with broken limbs, or epileptic fits. There's social work, as they talk to a mother who wants to make sure the school has no contact with an estranged father, or as they separate two warring families on the playground. In many schools, there's daily peacemaking between warring children.

There has to be, in some classrooms, expertise about different conditions. Some of these are natural, some socially constructed. In the first category, when I was in my last headship, a probationer (a Newly Qualifed Teacher, or NQT as she would be called today) was asked to supply valium anally to a child if she suffered an epileptic fit. What politician or lawyer, the day job brutally jettisoned, has such an acute duty in the first year of his or her career, while keeping 30 clients calm and safe?

In the second category, teachers are bombarded with

the need to know about conditions that seem to be restricted to social classes. AHDS is one example. Dyslexia is another. When did you last see a middle-class child diagnosed with the former, or a working-class child with the latter?

The tradition of teaching is noble because, like philosophy, science and poetry, it is a system of enquiry. It is about understanding. Among teachers, there's pre-eminently Jesus and his questions that put the other person in a place where learning might happen ('But whom say ye that I am?'), but that cause him to learn as well (whom will Peter say that Christ is?). His parables always yoke a truth about God to a truth about the life his listeners live.

And there's that other teacherly element in his work, his unremitting attention to the poor, the sick, the young and the outcasts. In all the yelling of the crowd, he focuses on the blind beggar, or the woman with a haemorrhage, or that other woman, gathering crumbs from his table, or that wicked little man, Zacchaeus, a man cheating his own people and working for the enemy, and now suddenly spotted by Jesus up a sycamore tree.

Like Christ, the teacher has to pay this kind of attention every day, and does so. Not with Christ's success, of course, but with his example in his or her mind. There's also Socrates and his questions. He doesn't tell the young men he corrupted (or so the state said) what is true, but he guides them to the truth through questions.

On the other hand, Shakespeare didn't think much of teachers. I wonder what he'd suffered at Stratford Grammar School. There is only one teacher in his works, Holofernes in *Love's Labour's Lost*. On his entry he displays his pompous pedantry, riddled with errors, that presumably were considered typical of his calling:

> The deer was, as you know, sanguis, in blood; ripe as the pomewater, who now hangeth like a jewel in the ear of coelo, the sky, the welkin, the heaven; anon falleth like a crab on the face of the terra, the soil, the land, the earth. (Act 4, Scene II)

To get an idea of this man's character, speak the speech in a voice always likely to descend to the irritable. He is determined to translate his Latin terms into various examples of English, as though this repetition will somehow teach his listeners. Two of the Latin words are wrong, by the way: another insight into Shakespeare's view of teachers. 'These Latin words . . . are the emblems of the pedant's (schoolmaster's) trade . . . they are dragged in' says Richard David in his edition of the play.

Reading novels like *Emma* and *The Last Chronicle of Barset*, one realizes how low in the public estimation, at least in England, the task of teaching had fallen. It is the job Jane Fairfax will have to do if she doesn't marry money. The poverty-stricken Grace Crawley works for a

8

pittance in a dames' school. We learn absolutely nothing of the schooling of men like Mr Darcy and Archdeacon Grantly. And poor Charlotte Brontë suffers in her school, with girls she sourly calls, in a letter home, 'fat-headed oafs' (Barker 1994).

It is only in the last 100 years that teaching has been made a profession, let alone respected by most people. And this will not have pleased that most teacher-like of writers, George Bernard Shaw, who dismissed the profession with a remark that has practically become axiomatic among the business community: 'He who can, does. He who cannot teaches' (from his essay 'Education' in *Maxims for Revolutionaries*, written by 'John Tanner'). One is forced to reflect that it's a privilege to serve a profession initiated by Confucius, Socrates, Christ, and others like them, and denigrated by George Bernard Shaw.

This book is about coping when things go wrong, specifically these:

♦ You get drunk, and have to teach the next day.

♦ You have an affair, or a marriage, that ends.

♦ You have a headteacher dominated by concerns not educational, but administrative and managerial.

♦ You work with colleagues who think teaching is a bore and a pain.

How to Teach with a Hangover

♦ You come face to face with the bestial visor of Ofsted.

♦ You encounter children's bad behaviour.

Most books about education quote other books about education. But what, you might say, do they of education know who only education know? This book will draw on fiction and poetry, in the belief that these arts will teach us, if we read and listen carefully, much about what we do in the classroom, much as they teach us about life.

Write

There is one strategy which always works for me, and it applies to all the problems, so I am going to offer it here: write.

You'll respond with 'he would say that'. But one of the best activities for dealing with any crisis in education (or anywhere else) is to get it down on paper, or on a screen. The problem is that the period during, or just after a crisis, is the last time we feel like writing. We want to pour a cup of tea, or go for a drink and share the problem with a colleague, or a non-colleague, or go on holiday, or to bed.

But at its lowest level, scribbling a list of things that have to be done is comforting. It means we have done something, and that we know the order in which the other things have to be done. We know that the tick we place by each task represents an achievement. But at a higher level, writing about a crisis is to make something, to create an object. When we see that object, we can reflect on it, we can think about it; the object is, obviously, related to the crisis, but it is tidier. It is, for the time being, perfect. We can comprehend this object, while we cannot (in either sense of the word, understand, or, literally 'get round') comprehend the experience we have undergone; the row with the head, for example, or with a teacher who seems not to care about the children.

Though writing and reading what we have written is not to understand, let alone to solve, our problem, the writing has given us steps, in the shape of words and sentences, that tighten our grip on it, that make it less likely to jump up suddenly and bite us while we are sleeping. To have written is to find some comfort.

But comfort is not a strong word. So let's ratchet the matter up. To write something down about a crisis is to enable ourselves to learn about that crisis. And while learning is not always comfortable, it at least leads us towards what is our perpetual aim, as teachers: the truth.

Not that you'd always know this. I'm writing as the schools round me prepare for Christmas, with all the sentimental lies about the Bible story doled out yet again in nativity plays, soppy music and ghastly displays. And there are the wider, year-long lies, too, that we as teachers are involved in: that children can be measured, that schools can be placed in league tables like football teams. But I anticipate . . .

Talk

This is so obvious that I nearly decided not to write it. A problem shared is not a problem halved, but it is a problem rendered less awful. Teachers should build a framework for supportive talk, especially early in their careers. Up to 20 years ago, conversations about practice were common in schools, because there was time for them. I remember sitting on desks in a colleague's classroom after the children had gone home during my early jobs, talking about individual children, about successes and failures, about parents, about the headteacher; comparing notes about lessons that had made me joyful or tearful.

Now, the sheer weight of administrative work – evaluating that, recording this, making this statement or preparing that policy (I read of one school that has a policy document for policy-making) – has not only taken teachers' time away: it has taken away the opportunities to talk, and, by extension, to criticize the regime in which they work. To load teachers down with tasks that are, by their nature, both sedentary and solitary, is a political act. It is to negate the chance of revolution, or indeed, evolution.

Teaching is a tough profession, especially when we are unfortunate enough to live in interesting times. But it is a glorious one, too, when everything we say has a chance of being remembered for a lifetime by one of our students. 'In a perfect world, everybody would want to be a teacher. Other jobs, like the President's, would be done by those who weren't good enough to teach.'

Enough of this. Let's go to the pub.

1 Teaching with a Hangover

Good faith, a little one; not past a pint, as I am a soldier.

Othello

. . . and he drank of the wine, and was drunken . . .

Genesis 9

How frank can I be? I submitted three proposals to my publisher. Two were serious. One I've forgotten, but the other was an idea for a book close to my heart: teaching in places other than classrooms. I had worked with children in the open air, in churches, in cathedrals and in a mosque; in the Bishop's Palace at Lincoln, and in Castle Acre Priory in Norfolk, and had seen work done – writing, drawing and model-making – by children in Barbara Hepworth's marvellous sculpture garden in St Ives, Cornwall. All the work had a life more evident than

15

it usually possesses when done in the confines of the classroom. A drawing lesson taught outside a school building rather than inside it produces results with a new dimension, simply because it makes the children look from a different perspective. And breathing the outdoor air is a stimulus to thought. It teaches not only art, but architecture, design and history.

But the publisher said no.

I also submitted a joke. Somehow email encourages this sort of off-the-cuff playing, and I suggested a book called *Teaching with a Hangover*. It's obvious now what happened. My son (training at the time as a primary teacher) was at home that day, and we worked out a framework that is the basis of this book. But what advice do I have to give about the classroom swimming in front of your eyes at 9am, the dry mouth, the foul breath, the vague but almost tangible guilt, the sense that there is a good life to be lived and that you are not living it, the feeling that the things you should do you don't, and things that you shouldn't do, you do?

It was called The White Hart, I remember. A parody of an English pub, it was in the middle of the high street in the old town of Stevenage in Hertfordshire. The landlord was an ex-military type called Bill. Old soldiers, or imitations of them, seemed to be obligatory for the running of pubs in those days, much as they were obligatory in the caretaking of schools. Bill had straight iron grey hair swept back, a glistening ruddy face, and a sizeable waistline. By closing time, he was sweating like a shire horse forced to run the Grand National. A non-commissioned officer, I reckon. One of those working-class types that had risen up the ladder as far as a lack of a public school and Sandhurst education would let them.

His wife, whose name I have forgotten, was heftily made up, with back-combed hair at a distance from both its original colour and her scalp. Now she would be taken for a pantomime dame, or possibly a drag act. Both were genial under all circumstances, and there were circumstances that required extreme geniality.

There were always jokes displayed behind the bar from holidaying drinkers, and most were of that peculiar English variety 'the dirty postcard'. 'With their endless succession of fat women in tight bathing dresses and their crude drawing and unbearable colours', they have been memorably celebrated by George Orwell (1961) in his article 'The Art of Donald McGill' in his *Collected Essays*.

I drank there at least two evenings a week in my first three years' teaching, but it was probably only two or three pints a night at most. There were better pubs up the road, serving local East Anglian beers. The Yorkshire Grey, for example, which had the treasured range of Greene King ales, and the Two Diamonds, a McMullens pub that looked too forbidding to enter: dark, small, with frosted windows, bars and tables lined with men with roll-ups and pints whose stares forbad entry to anyone but themselves or their kind. But I was yet to fall among the Campaign for Real Ale (CAMRA) members who were to complete my seduction into beer drinking.

I had an American girlfriend at the time. Jane. She was a student teacher, and her anglophile family had sent her over from Texas for a teaching practice, and she had landed in the school where I was working. She couldn't get over (of course) the fact that the English drank what she called 'warm' beer. Bill colluded with me that I would call my nightly drinks (and soon Jane's nightly drinks, too) 'pints of Slimmers'. Jane reappears in my chapter 'Kissing and Parting: Love and its Trials'.

Other evenings I studied for an Open University degree, a pioneer student for that noble concept of Harold Wilson's government. You can judge the relative ethics of that government and John Major's by noting that the former will be remembered for the OU, the latter for the National Lottery. After 34 years I can still remember my student number, A0022575. I ran a five-a-side football club, read novels and poetry; was involved in the local church.

Would I have time for all this if I were a young teacher today? For many of them, there will be not only no beer during the week, but no study, no intense reading, and almost no social life at all as they spend evenings filling in what Charles Causley so prophetically called in the 1950s 'useless bits of paper' ('School at four o'clock' in

Collected Poems, 1992). He had 'useless bits of paper' then? I'm glad for his sake that he wasn't teaching in the new millennium.

My first three years of teaching are memories of that new town, the roll-up blackboards in the first school, the children in my first class (many of whom I can still name), the football teams I ran, my first teaching of art, courses at other schools on music and movement, the teachers' centre . . . but they also include the hoppy, malty and faggy smell of The White Hart, and the Ind Coope brewer's sign on the outside. And Bill and his filthy humour.

I applied for deputy headship of a new school. The interviews took place twenty doors up from that pub, in The Grange, the local education office. The headteacher had, of course, already been appointed. He'd come, we were told, from a private school in Nassau, in the Bahamas. Doctrinaire to a fault, I wondered if I wanted to work for a private school teacher. Sheepishly, the candidates gathered in the little waiting room. I can remember one rival, a man about the same age as me. I'll call him Tom. We were swapping the usual chat about where we were teaching at the moment, where we'd trained and the like, when another candidate was ushered in. Tall, female, good looking, tanned. 'And where've you been working?' one of us asked. 'I've been a deputy in Nassau,' she said.

She got the job, of course. But better was to follow. At

How to Teach with a Hangover

5.30pm, restart for licensing hours in those days before pubs were thrown wide open all day, Tom and I were drinking a pint of beer each in another boozer, a huge, pretentious hotel called The Cromwell. Outside it was spring, in this gloomy cavern it was autumnal. In came the new head, his arm tenderly (as we saw it, and as I still see it) ushering in his deputy. There was a tableau when he saw us; embarrassment as tasty as over-salted chips.

He came over to us and offered us a drink. He addressed me first, and I accepted a follow up pint. My friend had had time to think, and he had more chutzpah than I've ever been able to summon, as well as a deeper knowledge of booze: 'A double rum and black, please,' he said. A small revenge, but both tasty and intoxicating.

I had discovered beer in Brixton. It was a half pint of mild, horrible to my palate, acidic and bitter (and, I know now, almost devoid of alcohol), but I knew then, straightaway, that I had to have more of it. To sit in a smoky room, its ceilings coloured a greyish terracotta with generations of smokers' smoke, became a necessity at least once or twice a week. But I never went so far as that character Books Do Furnish a Room Bagshaw, in Anthony Powell's twelve-volume sequence of novels *A Dance to the Music of Time*, who felt no day was worth living unless he was on licensed premises at closing time.

College days were, of course, days of alcoholic excess. They still are, as far I can judge from watching my son and his friends. Rumours of what the rugby fifteen got up to with soda siphons and meaningless songs ('I see a zoomba, zoomba, zoomba . . .') after a victory on the field against Loughborough terrified me so much that I was never in a bar, knowingly, with more than one of them present. The idea of dancing trouserless on a bar table while my mates poured lagers down their necks made me queasy: it still does.

But in the city centre, my friend David introduced me to the delights of Berni inns. This was a chain of restaurants that mimicked classy establishments, but were really cheap chophouses. I remember dim reddish lighting and underpaid, slightly surly waiters. The menu started with tiny schooners of sherry and continued with prawn cocktails, an exotic concoction for working-class lads brought up on strong tea and tinned Crosse and Blackwell soup.

It went through any food you liked as long as it was cheap meat grilled to a crisp, and ended with Irish coffee: a magical black glass with a Guinness-like head that contained instant coffee, brown sugar, a shot of John Jameson's and cream. Oh boy, were we living now. The waiter poured the cream expertly over the back of a spoon, and it lodged on the top of the drink. There it was, an emblem of our emancipation from our upbringing, as clean and white and pure as a clerical collar. Tinned spaghetti hoops and tubs of ersatz coleslaw, all the afterbirth of the Second World War and its resultant austerity, would never hold the same magic again.

Today, many of the students I meet have been inducted into the business of drinking in their early teens with the cynical manufacturers' ploy of mixing liquor with sweets. The very names make anyone of my generation blench. A hangover produced by a dozen Barcardi Breezers, with all the chemicals cocktailed into the cheap rum, must be a different matter from a hangover induced by bitter beer. And, in any case, the sheer quantity of beer, drunk as it is in pints, combined with its relative weakness, militates against excess. The bladder says no before the alcohol hits the brain. Or it does for me. Binge drinking, a current panic as I write, is caused in part by the fact that it is possible to consume massive amounts of alcohol in a short time. And in the long time offered by 24-hour opening, you can get drunk in whatever way your metabolism takes you: sloppy-drunk, maudlin-drunk or fighting-drunk.

The only times I was in a pub at closing time were in The Swan in Berkhamsted, where I had a deputy headship, and later a headship. My artist friend Alastair and I would be dragooned out of the place by the camp Cockney barman, who would call out at 10.30pm: 'Ain't you got no 'omes to go to? Anyone 'ere in five minutes will 'ave to sleep wiv me.'

Picture two young male primary school teachers. It is the day in early September before the school year starts.

This annual beginning has extra tension, which involves extra beer, because there is a new headteacher in the school, called (say) Robinson. The two young men had crawled along their high street from The Goat at one end to the Crooked Billet at the other. I happen to know this high street. It involves, apart from The Goat and The Crooked Billet, The Bull, The Swan, The King's Arms, The Lamb and The Crown. It's a trail through yeoman England, with the names, never mind the beer.

Working with a new headteacher is a crisis in itself, as you speculate quietly on what type he or she will be (see Chapter 3) and the words 'new' and 'broom' and 'sweep' and 'clean' are never far from anyone's thoughts, and you gaze dourly on the weakest parts of your practice: leaving an autumn display on the wall till the following autumn, say, or shouting at the children, or writing 'v.g.' or 'see me' on their work, hoping that it is a suitable response.

The two young men, bleary the next morning, silence their respective classes. 'Frighten them early' was a received wisdom in those days among some teachers. 'You can always soften up later when you've got them where you want them.' One of the young men writes a note to his friend (Robertson, say – anyway, not Robinson – pay attention at the back), puts it in an envelope, and seals it. 'Take this to Mr Robertson, please' he said to a child.

How to Teach with a Hangover

Children are always grateful to get out of the class-room, especially one where they have been traumatized by a new teacher, possibly their first man insisting on Total Silence While I Do The Register, I Do Not Want To Hear A Pin Drop after the relative kindness of women in the infant department. In any case, a little stroll along a corridor, or across the yard to a mobile classroom, is a touch of real life, in contrast to the four walls that are often a prison of varying unpleasantness. You get to see the milkman's van, or the postman, or a police car tear-ing down the street and you can smirk secretly at friends in other classes.

But this child is carrying a little bomb, a note that says 'I'm bored, you wanker. Amuse me'. And, of course, the child takes it to the new headteacher, Robinson, not Robertson. I hope you've been paying attention. Ques-tion for management course. What should the clever headteacher do? Let the teacher sweat on it for a few days, and then say, primly, 'I destroyed your note'? Call him in at coffee time and give him a rollicking? Amuse him, as requested?

He did the first. A really cool new head would have done the third, of course.

How To Deal With Hangovers

In his excellent book *On Drink*, Kingsley Amis (1972) addresses the hangover issue with characteristic wit. Unfortunately, he bases all his cures on the assumption that you have nothing else to do for the rest of the day, except to recover to the point where you can add some paragraphs to your current novel. So lying in as long as possible, and then eating a breakfast like Churchill's – one brace cold snipe, one pint port (Churchill thought a meal worthless unless he smoked and drank before, during and after it); or Horatio Bottomley's – one pair kippers, one tumbler brandy and water; or Coleridge's – six fried eggs, one glass laudanum and seltzer (laudanum being alcoholic tincture of opium) – are not open to you, because you know in your heart that a hangover is not a justifiable reason for staying off work. You have to face your class, your colleagues, parents, the headteacher or possibly an inspector. Churchill only had a war to run. In any case, you are not ill, dammit, you are stupid.

Nor are modern hangover cures open to us: raw eggs in milk and vodka with Worcester sauce, for example. Those three breakfasts and that cure are part of the 'hair of the dog' cure system, which I think is insane. It's like being bitten by a dog and then asking a dog to bite you the next morning . . . no, sorry, I've got it now. It's like being run over the night before, and then being asked to

25

be run over the next morning. Sorry. Oh, I was so drunk last night.

Amis's most helpful offering in this area is that there are two hangovers. One, the more obvious one, is the physical hangover. You feel terrible. Head aches. Limbs are exhausted. Throat feels (as a friend of mine at college used to say, obscurely but appositely enough) 'like a yak's jockstrap'. 'I'll never drink again' you keep repeating. One teacher kept saying, 'Sorry, sorry, sorry'. I said, 'There's no need to apologize to me' and he cut in bitterly: 'I'm not apologizing to you. I'm apologizing to myself.'

But there is also a metaphysical hangover. You feel guilty at subjecting your body to this beating. After all, it is, as St Paul (more of whom later) says, the temple of the Holy Spirit. It deserves at least the love and attention that the Dean and Chapter give their cathedral. Instead, you have treated it like a squalid squat. You are right to feel guilty. You also feel guilty, or you should, about your partner, your children, if you have any. They live at a significant distance from your problem, but they are still close enough to suffer from it.

For what it's worth, here are some ways of dealing with a hangover before teaching. I warn you that my latent puritanism emerges in this section.

Drink lots and lots of water, because you are dehydrated. Orange juice is also good. Black coffee isn't good, as it irritates the liver, but it does feel as if it's good (much as the booze felt as if it was good for you last night).

If you can stand it, and if you can afford the time, cook a breakfast.

Get in a walk in the open air, even if it is the walk to work. You shouldn't drive anyway, because you are almost certainly still over the limit. A story makes this clear. A poet gives a reading some 20 miles from his home. Having drunk beer and whisky during and after the reading, he gets into his car and (and this is unusual in the seriously drunk driver, to judge from newspaper reports) realizes he can't drive. So he books in at a B & B to sleep it off. Oh, he must have felt, as he woke. I feel terrible. I will drink water, lie here for a while contemplating my sins. Eat eggs and bacon, drink coffee. Then I will be all right. He is pulled up by the police in the morning, breathalysed and banned for a year.

Acknowledge your guilt, and pray for forgiveness. Quoting that St Paul verse I referred to earlier is a good idea here: 'For the good that I would I do not; but the evil which I would not, that I do' (Romans 7). For the classically minded, it is worth noting that Ovid wrote something similar to this, and before St Paul: 'I see the better way, and approve it; I follow the worse' in his *Metamorphoses*. Ovid may have suffered hangovers; I think it unlikely of St Paul, though he did recommend taking a little wine for thy stomach's sake.

During morning assembly (assuming you are not in

How to Teach with a Hangover

charge of it) close your eyes and contemplate your wickedness. Here is a litany I have composed for this eventuality:

Lord I am not worthy

to take a job scraping chewing gum off the streets, let alone take charge of these children.

Lord I am not worthy

to murmur at strangers 'Coppers for a cup of tea?' let alone take charge of these children.

Lord I am not worthy

to chair an editorial meeting at the *Daily Mail*, let alone take charge of these children.

Lord I am not worthy
Lord I am not worthy
Lord I am not worthy

If more than one of you in school is hungover, say this together in a quiet moment in the staffroom, saying the repeated clauses in unison, and the central clauses in one voice. The litany should go on as long as time and the memory of things you are not worthy to do persist. Make sure there are no parents, governors or inspectors nearby, unless any of them want, or need, to join in.

A Letter to Send to a Colleague Who Has Been Out Drinking the Night Before Teaching

Teachers Drinking Moderately

[Here should follow a convincing looking address, phone number, email address, website, etc.]

Dear Mr/Ms

You may have heard of my work concerned with persuading young people against the evils of strong drink.

I give lectures in public halls, and have, until recently, been accompanied by an old acquaintance, Clive, who would sit on the stage, leering at the more attractive specimens of both sexes, belching, breaking wind, and heckling me with oaths and abuse.

Clive would sing drinking songs such as 'Show me the way to go home' and 'I belong to Glasgow' in a quavery but forceful light baritone.

With his rose-coloured, misshapen nose and his slobber-infested lips, his appearance was a strong incentive against excess. His staggering walk from the wings and, occasionally, over the edge of the stage on to the front rows of the audience, taught all who were present a powerful lesson.

How to Teach with a Hangover

Unfortunately, last month Clive died.

Certain mutual friends of ours have suggested you as his possible replacement. If you are interested in this good work, please apply to me at the above address etc., etc. . . . .

Yours faithfully

The 20th and 21st verses of the ninth chapter of Genesis tell the tale of the effect of drink. Not many Sunday School children are told this story. Noah was previously, with his ark, the saviour of good humankind as opposed to wicked humankind. Everyone knows about the ark and the animals going up the gangplank two by two. It is probably (apart from the nativity narrative in St Luke's Gospel) the last familiar Bible story. Noah was under the instructions of God, and he was the only human to whom God spoke. He had a rainbow in the sky for a solemn promise, surely one of the loveliest presents anyone has ever received. He was the man who had everything, and now he even had a rainbow.

Then, in a few words, a secret to those Sunday School children, he descends breathtakingly: 'And Noah began to be an husbandman, and he planted a vineyard: and he drank of the wine, and was drunken; and he was uncovered within his tent.' From tyro wine grower to drunken self-exposer inside a few words. Scary.

I began this chapter with a quotation from *Othello*.

Teaching with a Hangover

After this remark, poor Cassio is seduced into a stupor by Iago with a song:

> And let me that canakin clink, click;
> And let me that canakin clink;
> A soldier's a man
> O life's but a span;
> Why, then, let a soldier drink.

Cassio replies: 'Fore God, an excellent song' (Act 2, Scene III).

Take out the word 'soldier' and replace it with 'teacher'; get seduced by that song: downfall. You can get to the bottom, like Noah, in 28 words.

Teaching with a hangover? Forget it. There are ways of dealing with the things, but they don't convince me, and they won't help you. I often reflect that, had I not discovered mild ale and the earnest *Guardian* in my late teens, and stuck to water and the dubious moral certainty of the *Telegraph*, I'd be a richer, more easy-going man today; though you might need a pint when confronted with the predicament in my next chapter, or some of the headteachers in the one after that.

2 Kissing and Parting: Love and its Trials

*Since ther's no helpe, Come let us kisse and
part . . .*

Michael Drayton (1563–1631)

The scene is yet another English pub. It is some time in
the early 1970s, but no matter, kissing and parting are
timeless activities, as Michael Drayton's lovely clear sonnet from 1619 demonstrates. I have printed it with its
original punctuation and spelling, because that helps us
to speak it aloud, and points up a distance between the
time when it was written and our time. Note below the
nouns and pronouns that he capitalizes: some are capit-
alized because of contemporary convention, some for
other reasons. Note the force acquired by the separation
of 'my' and 'Selfe', and the pathos effected by the cap-
itals on 'Cancell' and 'Vowes'. As Seamus Heaney has
written somewhere, one should taste a poem as well as

33

hear and see it. Speak it, hinting at those 'e's at the end of words like 'Vowes' and 'Browes'.

The poem continues:

> Nay, I have done: You get no more of Me,
> And I am glad, yea glad withall my heart,
> That thus so cleanly, I my Self can free,
> Shake hands forever, Cancell all our Vowes,
> And when We meet at any time againe,
> Be it not seene in either of our Browes,
> That We one jot of former Love reteyne; . . .

Jane is the American student from Chapter 1, and she is sitting with me in the pub, drinking her last pint of English beer. She had got her degree, and had flown to her parents' beloved England for a teaching practice that's part of an American post-graduate qualification. And her teaching practice has been in my classroom! We've taught together, and photographed each other and the class of children in front of displays we'd spent hours arranging.

And during that spring term we have fallen in love. I have inducted her into the ways of English beer at The White Hart in Stevenage, shown her round Cambridge and other places. She has been transported, in both senses of the word, by my little Morris 1000, and its smell of leather seats and petrol. I have seen snowdrops and forsythia and cherry blossom and *old buildings* ('Look at those old buildings!') with American eyes.

But now she is going home. I have driven her to within a mile of the house of an adviser where she is to spend her last night in England. Tomorrow she will fly back to the States. But what a sense of humour these American girls have! Suddenly, she stands, walks over to the silent juke box . . . and within seconds we are listening to Peter, Paul and Mary's 'Leaving on a Jet Plane': 'All my bags are packed, I'm ready to go . . .' and I am crying in the corner of an empty saloon bar, unmindful of the regulars. And so is she.

Parting is the very stuff of cliché, of course, but only because the realities of it are there for all of us to feel at some time or another. Here, in the Jane story, are the pop record, the two drinks on a tray, and the aeroplane.

Much later, Jane sent me an anthology of American poems, and wrote in it, in that cursive style favoured by her people, 'America waits for you in Conroe Texas'. Then she married, and was killed with her husband in a car crash. Their disabled baby son survived. I had a snap of her in my wallet for a few years, until it was stolen from my jacket as it hung on my chair in the office where I had my first headship. The police found the wallet, stripped of a fiver or two, but with her picture there, stained with the urine from the public lavatory where it had been thrown.

Philip Larkin (1988) tells us, and all the evidence suggests he is right, that 'where desire takes charge, readings may grow erratic' ('Deceptions'). Love endangers us, through its very unpredictability, though we don't realize it when it strikes so sweetly, and with such certainty.

Love and sex, notoriously, are related, but they are not, equally notoriously, the same thing. The latter, in Kingsley Amis's typically blunt words, 'is a momentary itch' [while] 'love never lets you go'. I remember that first line as an even blunter one ('Sex stops when you pull up your pants'), but either Amis changed the line since the poem's first publication, or my memory is faulty. Either way, I prefer the cruder version.

Love, when it becomes a problem, makes you do things that you don't want to do. It makes you keep silence in pain, act decently against all provocation, forswear revengeful thinking and, indeed, action. It is constant in the face of inconstancy. St Paul had sussed it out. Love (which was translated 'charity' in the Authorised Version) 'suffereth long, and is kind; . . . envieth not; vaunteth not itself, is not puffed up. Doth not behave itself unseemly, seeketh not her own, is not easily provoked, thinketh no evil . . .' (1 Corinthians: 13).

And the speaker of Shakespeare's sonnets, in the face, apparently, of sexual horrors – his male lover has seduced, or been seduced by his female one – solemnly tells us, in lines that have a quasi-religious significance for me, that 'love is not love/Which alters when it alteration finds' (Sonnet 116). The love that alters can't have been love in the first place. Your love won't alter. If it was love, it still is, in spite of whatever happens.

Sex, on the other hand, makes you do things, or persuades you to do things, that you know you shouldn't. In Larkin's poem, the desire is about rape, and while I hope and largely believe that rape is something few teachers experience, the passions of sex without love – the word exploitation seems to sum them up – are something with which most of us are familiar. Exploitation can be less dramatic, of course; there is a kind of emotional irresponsibility that toys with the affections of others.

Readings grow even more erratic when desire on one side ceases to take charge, when it groweth cold, when what is still central to one person becomes peripheral to the other. When, to use the teenage vernacular that has, as far as I know, neither changed nor been bettered for a generation or two, you dump someone, or get dumped. Here, truly, we are really in the dark. The evenings and nights are terrible, especially in the winter, but we have to turn up at school, and face a class, and do the best we can.

It doesn't matter much, practically, whether we are the dumper or the dumped. Indeed, to be dumped is easier, because in our experience we encompass all the first-hand pain. The one who inflicts the pain knows that it is terrible, but not how terrible it is. He – or she – can only guess. That guessing is sleep-depriving.

How to Teach with a Hangover

Few things are more destructive of the working life of a teacher than crises that come from love's crises.

During my first teaching job, I started going out with a colleague. Though (or perhaps because) the affair was intense, it didn't last long, and when we came to the last evening, which was far more beer- and wine-fuelled than any other evening we'd shared, the end was bitter and noisy.

Next morning we were both late for school. It was obvious to the wily headteacher what had happened. It would have been obvious to any headteacher. I don't know what he said to her, but to me he said that my private life shouldn't interfere with my professional one. I think now that this advice, though commonsensical, is impossible to follow, especially if you enjoy teaching so much (as I did, as I do) that it stands strong as a part of your life. And personal or professional don't matter, it's just your life. But I remember I apologized, and said it wouldn't happen again. It didn't.

How to Deal with These Crises

The secret, when your life is, or appears to be (and they are one and the same thing at the time), falling apart is to live in the present. Or as Jesus puts it, to live knowing that 'sufficient unto the day is the evil thereof'. Because, when a love affair, a long-term relationship or a marriage ends, it is difficult to concentrate on goals to be reached. I mean goals like, What will I do at Christmas? and Where will I go on holiday? and How will I survive without her or him?

Everyday things become a cause for sighing. Getting a haircut, booking the car in for a service, planning a meal, especially if, after all the years, it is, with a sickening jolt, a meal for one; all these become as big as beating the Aussies in a test match in Melbourne, or redecorating the house in a single day, or founding a political party with social justice as its main aim, and sustaining it without its decaying inside a year.

The only solution is to think of the goals that have to be reached today, to list them, as I have already suggested; then to achieve them; and then to celebrate them when you've done it. These can be negative goals, like not drinking a four pack or a bottle of cheap red, or not leaving the washing up in the sink overnight. And they can be positive ones like changing the duvet cover, cleaning the bathroom, cooking rather than getting a takeaway and roasting rather than frying.

Food is critical. Coming home to a dark cold flat or house is dispiriting. To think about cooking and eating is difficult, and there are so many other things to do, like turning the heating on, feeding the cat, opening the junk mail, checking the answerphone and the emails, usually finding there is nothing new. But when all these things are done, cooking a proper meal rather than a fry-up will reap rewards. You will have made something. You are still capable of creativity, even at a low level. Like the writing I recommended in the Introduction, the meal is an object that you have made. It is a little work of art, temporary as it is. That makes you feel better. Also, your blood sugar level was low, and that makes you sad.

And school! You feel that you are pushing your way through your work, as though, somehow you've had to get behind yourself, and shove, and shove, and shove. Even the little things are difficult, like taking the register, because there is really only one item on your agenda, and everything else, even the children – or especially the children – are a distraction who should be in Any Other Business, and nodded through without discussion.

Advice From The Front

My friend, a headteacher, gave me an account of a crisis in his life. His wife left him. How did he cope?

I made lists, and ticked them off. Anything around the house that needed mending, I mended it if I could, or rang someone up, and they mended it, and then I went on to the next thing on the list, and mended it, or got someone to mend it. It mattered for my morale. I didn't want to become a slob, and I thought that the possibility was all too present.

The oven had been dodgy for a while, and we [he and his wife] had done nothing about it, so I went out to Bennett's and bought an oven. I'd done something without her! And something she'd delayed doing, for whatever reason! I can't do practical things mostly, but I found an old college friend, and we'd done it, fitted the oven within two hours. Him doing the clever stuff, me doing, or helping with, the humping about, the carrying. She'd only been gone a day and a bit, and already I had a gleaming new oven, with a light and a window that allowed me to see what was cooking. I roasted potatoes straightaway, I watched the edges browning, and I felt better . . .

I remember sweeping the dust away from where the old oven had been, and thinking, that's something done, this place is better now . . .

The next night I felt like I wanted to die, waking up, knowing I was alone, and it had been 15 years, and thinking about all the holidays, Greece, Spain, Malta, Italy, France, but in the morning, the oven, I know this sounds pathetic, cheered me up. I went out to the garage with the photo albums, and put them where I couldn't see them. Later, I thought, when I can face catching glimpses of us on beaches, I'll put them into bin liners and tie them up to stop them getting mildewed . . .

I needed to look better. She'd bought all my clothes, mostly from second-hand shops, but I opened an account at Coe's, and got my hair cut . . .

I found there was a temptation not to shower, just to wash hurriedly. A big mistake! You feel so much better if you'd showered and shaved. I bought smelly things, cologne and the like, that I'd never bothered with before. For a while, I suspect, I smelt like a badger, then like a male brothel . . .

I realized that I had been looking forward to growing old with my wife. I found myself saying to her absence, 'I was looking forward to growing old with you'. I wasn't going to do that now, and that upset me more than I can say. I remember thinking, with a great horror, I don't want to die alone.

I remember the turning point. I thought, You are my past, you are a memory . . .

I need someone to grow old with. A friend said to me, go on evening classes, join a choir, meet women. Don't do Spanish, that's full of old people looking to retire to the Costa del Sol . . .

It is important to talk to people, you can't afford pride. Though you feel like a leper, like an amputee, like your guts have been ripped out, and think that everyone is looking at you because of what has happened, they aren't. Millions of people have been through this . . .

Anyway, there are hundreds of people in your town like you. It happened to me just before Christmas, and I thought every family in town walking home with parcels and trees and the like was perfect, only mine was breaking up. I talked to people, and heard the most horrendous stories, most of them, I felt, even worse that mine . . .

If you haven't been gregarious, change. Go to parties you normally avoid . . .

You have to get used to the fact that there will be a period every day when you are very low, two or three hours in my case, but also that the gloom will lift when you remember what you have done. And that you are not solely definable in terms of the rejection that you face, that you are dealing with. That you can be defined by your success in other ways, your hobbies, your job, whatever . . .

One day, I decided, I will wake up, and rejection won't be the first thought . . .

How to Teach with a Hangover

Before that stage in recovery, there will be another. There will be a stateliness. 'A formal feeling comes' is how Emily Dickinson puts it. There will be a stone-like acceptance, a mechanical proceeding across the world. And this proceeding will, if you stay sober, have a great, if injured, dignity. It will be an 'Hour of lead.'

And there will be yet another stage. The Drayton sonnet I began with, like any English sonnet, has another six lines. You've seen the octet. Here is the sestet. Read it aloud, slowly, letting that final 'e' on 'speechlesse' linger slightly:

> Now at the last gaspe, of Loves latest Breath,
> When, his Pulse fayling, Passion speechlesse lies,
> When Faith is kneeling by his bed of Death,
> And Innocence is closing up his Eyes,
> Now if thou would'st, when all have given him over,
> From Death to Life, thou might'st him yet recover.

But it doesn't ring true. He had to write a sonnet, and get those last six lines in for structural reasons. He spoiled the poem.

No. Face it. It's over.

3 Teaching with a Dodgy Headteacher

Headmasters have powers at their disposal with which Prime Ministers have never yet been invested.
Winston Churchill, *My Early Life*

'Dodgy keep-pah', football crowds shout as the opposition goalie takes a goal kick, hoping he'll belt the ball to one of their players, or at least into the stands. What about dodgy headteachers?, I thought one day at Portman Road, the home of my team, as the Stoke keeper punted a ball into the dugouts for the fifth time. This chapter is about dodgy bosses.

The Person Headteacher

But first there is a species I am going to call, for want of a better term, 'the person headteacher'. In the 1960s and 1970s, it was fashionable to talk of 'child-centred education', and few of us (I didn't) saw an obvious flaw in this. The cliché ignored everyone else involved in teaching, such as parents and the teachers themselves. In those days, there were few teaching assistants (in Hertfordshire, for some reason, they were called 'welfare workers'), but the term ignored them as well.

The heads I am describing are not merely 'child-centred', because they show in countless ways that they are in the school, not only for the children, but also for you and your colleagues, whether other teachers or teaching assistants. Other heads pretend to be there for these reasons. They act the part. But the person headteacher really is in the job for the people, and they flicker in and out of this chapter.

These people often show signs of genial eccentricity, like George Harpole in J. L. Carr's *The Harpole Report*. He liked to surprise everyone at assembly occasionally by announcing 'Summer suns are glowing' at Christmas, or 'Silent Night' in the summer. Another headteacher turned a class's educational television programme off for the duration of the 2.30pm from Haydock Park. Another held three fingers up during assembly and said to the children, 'I have two important things to say to you today'. Such people are people heads, because what they are as people is what they are as headteachers.

The Other Headteachers

But I am mainly concerned with headteachers who are less concerned with human beings. It's not much of an exaggeration to say that every school has an enemy to innovation and creativity. It's a certainty to say that it isn't the children. It isn't the teachers, either, mostly – though see Chapter 4 on cynical colleagues. It's almost a certainty to say that it isn't the caretaker, or the cook, even though both of these people often hold more power in a school than might be expected. No young teacher should ever offend either of them. Is the school clean? Are the lunches decent?

It probably isn't the governing body, slaving away without pay over tiresome documents, or the parents. It isn't even, primarily (though I'm less certain about this) a succession of philistine governments, perversely equating learning with what can be measured in tests, and judging a school's quality by its position in league tables.

The main enemy to innovation and creativity is, as a character in an Alan Bennett play (*The History Boys*) says, the headteacher. Bennett is brilliant at headmasters, as they always are in his plays. In *Forty Years On*, played originally by John Gielgud, the head keeps breaking into public prayer ('if I don't say a prayer now no-one else will'). When his deputy (about to become his successor) goes 'too far' with his lavatorial jokes in the school play, the headmaster complains that the deputy is constantly 'putting ideas into the boys' heads'. 'Isn't that what education is supposed to be about?' says the deputy. The headmaster responds, 'I have always preferred the word "schooling" to "education" '.

Education is, according to me, more about the 'boys' being allowed to develop their own ideas, through conversations with their teachers. Jeeves (rather improbably, but quite correctly) confides to Bertie Wooster, with a surprising knowledge of Latin etymology, that 'education is a drawing out, not a putting in' (quoted in Rae 1991).

This schooling/education matter is a critical distinction. To 'school' children is to make them amenable. It is to make sure that they (as the police used to say in bad movies) 'come quietly', if not silently, into assembly. It is to make sure that, when they are 4 or 5 years old, they know that what sounds like a question ('Would you like to come and sit on the carpet?') is, in fact, an order. You can't say no, without a telling off. You might well be labelled 'awkward' or worse. Whenever they've heard questions like that at home, they've been real questions: 'Would you like some more potatoes?' Though nobody ever explains to the children why what sounds like a question at home is an order at school.

In the jargon of the educational psychologists of a few years ago, it is to 'socialize' them. This is to bend them to the ways of the school and, by extension, to the ways of society. It is, frankly, to institutionalize them. That's an ugly word for an ugly thing. A prisoner, or an army recruit, is institutionalized. 'When I blow the whistle, stand completely still. When I blow it again, move silently to your class lines . . .' You might as well be on the parade ground. Headteachers have a pivotal role to play in all this socialization. But they could have another role: not to school at all, or if it is absolutely necessary, to do it with a light touch. And to educate.

In state schools, headteachers have the wherewithal to stand in the way of the rubbish lobbed at schools, or at least to counter its worst effects. Instead, all too often, they actively encourage the managers rather than the people who matter – teachers, learning support assistants, children – by selling out: joining the National Association of Headteachers, and policing the worst idiocies of the politicians, such as the timings of the literacy hour; indeed, the whole reduction of the teaching of language to that dreary thing, literacy, and the reduction of mathematics to that equally dreary thing, numeracy.

Headteachers can be concerned with schooling, or with education. The former is to be a cynical hired hand.

How to Teach with a Hangover

The second is to set minds free. Not to put ideas into the children's head, but to allow the heads to generate their own ideas.

I was a headteacher three times, but eventually they found out. I was appointed to my first headship when I was 29. I was single, and I still had political and moral priggishness and adolescent acne. I took up the post when I was 30, and the acne hadn't cleared up. It was a few years before the priggishness cleared up, as well. I knew, I just *knew*, what a school should be like. It had to place writing at its centre, especially creative writing, especially poetry; and it had to take art seriously, too. I had glimmers of a belief that language was central, because you couldn't teach any subject without it. And in fact you were always teaching it, whatever you were teaching on the face of things. But it was years later before I developed this, and began to think of language as a means of learning everything, and saw how central it was in physical education, say, or mathematics.

And art? It made the building look good and impressed my elders and betters, the advisers who visited occasionally, far less often than inspectors do today. I had not a glimmer of the importance of art as a teacher; that, as Shaw says somewhere, 'it is the only teacher except torture'. So I proceeded to make that school as much like I thought any school should be. At the union meetings that took place in halls in the area, I saw that other schools were different, and secretly despised their displays, largely designed by the teachers, and their children's writing, which seemed to consist of copyings out of poetry, and their formal classrooms with all the children facing the front. Had these people not seen the Plowden Report?

Much later, I was to meet a headteacher who said that a school should be 'an extension of the headteacher's personality'. I thought that's all very well if the headteacher is a combination of Jesus, Leonardo and Shakespeare, but suppose he is a villain? Or, much more likely, a small-minded bureaucrat relieved to have largely escaped from immediate responsibility for the children?

I had been aiming at leading a school based on, if not my personality, my interests. Good job, I probably reflected later, that I'm a decent bloke. The idea (if that is not too grand a name for it) is what philosophers would call 'solipsistic', a view of the world, or a part of it, my school (note that 'my') based on me and my interests.

I was a dodgy keeper. I was obsessed, I would have said, with the arts. But in fact, I was concerned with the way a school should look: with display. For many years I had taught art, and spent hours pinning up the works, mostly painting, that the children had done. I am not proud of the way I worked then. I was a child of the Plowden generation, but few of us had read that report carefully. Instead, we were influenced by, and based our practice on, the photographs in it: snapshots of children (this was critical to all of us) arranged around desks so that they could talk to each other, rather than arranged in lines facing the blackboard, which acted as a kind of secular altar. Not for nothing was one of the best books of the period about English teaching called *The Disappearing Dais* (Whitehead 1966).

While much was inspiring in Plowden-influenced schools, there were problems. Frequently more money was spent on the material used to display work than was spent on the materials the children actually worked with. And often, more time was spent arranging a display than was spent in teaching the work that went into it. This was window-dressing. One adviser used the word 'pleasing' in connection with displays of art, which seemed to me, even then, a weak notion for art. You wouldn't use it about Beethoven's Ninth, or *King Lear*, or a Leonardo drawing; it seems insulting to use it about children's art.

I hope and believe that my ideas of art deepened, to include thinking about the process through which children travelled as they drew, painted and modelled, rather than just the product; I came to see children's art as an exploration of a relationship between the artist, his or her materials, and the world he or she lived in.

Today, when I think of headteachers, I still concentrate on how they relate to the expressive arts – poetry and drawing especially, but also dance, drama, music, painting and model-making. This is partly because my main interests are in these areas, but also because they present an interesting challenge. Every head must represent authority and order: everyone, even the most radical educationist, wants the children to be safe, and requires certain decorum in a school. There is something in this that is antagonistic to art, which requires risk, when order, sometimes, is only produced out of a chaos that is without form and void.

While the arts also represent an authority – teachers have to pass on the culture of previous generations – they are also subversive, because art, in looking for the truth, looks where other people don't look, where they are too frightened or too lazy to look. The headteacher has the difficult job of both maintaining authority and decorum, and of encouraging the arts in the search for the truth beneath surfaces. And it is not a matter of compromise: there has to be the maximum order for safety's and decorum's sake, and the maximum scope for innovation.

Were I a science, a religious education or a history teacher, there would also be this conflict of interest. They too are concerned with the truth. But I see the problem clearest in terms of the arts, with their way of insisting to managers that we – the writers, the painters, the dancers – are human beings, and not merely names on a checklist, or a league table.

In my present job, I meet about 100 primary school headteachers every year. The variety is impressive. Some, at one extreme, are tied by invisible ankle chains to their computer workstation, protected by a secretary. ('He's in a meeting . . .' 'She's very busy . . .') They only emerge from the office to drink coffee in the staffroom or, blinking at natural light, to bawl at some raucous Year 6s who have kicked a football through a window. At the other extreme, there are those whose behaviour shows that they are only there for the people in their school: the children, first, then the teachers, the non-teaching staff and the parents. These people can be seen all day long listening to children.

In my experience, the non-person heads break down into three camps. First, there are the computer headteachers. Second, there are the management headteachers; and finally, there are the bullies.

The Computer Headteachers

Soldiers in this sizeable army have been freed from any educational contact with children (or any contact at all, especially emotional contact) by successive governments' legislation. What has distressed most teachers – the forms, the endless preparation and evaluation – has been a joy to them. They don't have to teach. They have to read documents and respond to them. They have to know the acronyms of the current governmental obsessions, and these acronyms mean more to them than the names of the children in the school. They have to be computer literate, and literate in current political jargon (the courses that they've attended would fill a real teacher's CV) but knowledge of children no longer matters. They know the way governments talk and write. They're proud of their fluency in this opaque language. They're proficient in those phrases about 'rolling out programmes of reform' and the like. They know everything there is to know about tests.

But to know about tests is not to know about the children who have to sit them in the summer term, and how they feel about that experience. Then the sun shines warmly on the trees, and casts shadows on the grass and the paths, and the children are imprisoned, away from that sun, away from those trees, away from those shadows, away from that grass, away from those paths. The computer headteachers know nothing about that isolation from life. They have forgotten about sitting exams. Neither do they know or care anything about the teachers who administer the tests, almost always against their consciences.

Of course, the computer heads don't admit to this dark secret joy, this love of document and cursor and email and CD-ROM, this avoidance of children and teachers and parents. They don't admit it, not even to each other. To do that – even at that strange, quasi-masonic event, the heads' meeting – would be suicide to a reputation. Instead, they complain loud and long about the way in which their paperwork has isolated them from the children and even the staff. How well they remember the happy times teaching English or art or PE or whatever! 'Those were the days, when I actually had time to teach – and teaching is what I came into this profession for!'

No they didn't. They came into teaching because, although they sensed that they had neither the right kind of intelligence nor the raw courage for a life in business, they quite fancied business and all it implied, the not doing things, but, instead, the telling of other people to do them. And now successive Tory and Labour governments, vying with each other, notwithstanding their dishonest rhetoric, to be as much like the other side as possible, have turned their jobs into – businesses! They can be business managers, without profit and loss implications (although they have started to arrive – I hear frightening stories of schools being encouraged by authorities to invest in the stock market). They can tell people to do things. They're pigs in clover, they're the cats that got the cream, they've got it made. The computer headteacher is the real headteacher of today.

Even before the slow incessant white avalanche of legislation first appeared in the mountains of government, sometime in the late 1970s, these headteachers, or their predecessors, kept as far away from the children as they could. They doubled up classes when a teacher was ill, they had meeting after meeting with anyone who came to school and they attended meetings outside school with the religiosity of a hypocrite at Mass.

You can identify the computer heads by their clothes. They wear suits and shirts that would be rendered ready for Sketchley's if they went within 100 yards of Year 4 during their exuberant art lessons involving glue and paint with that newly qualified teacher. She still has the flame of freedom in her heart, and the light of science in her eyes. She knows that mess is good. These headteachers are frightened of the nursery, where, they have heard, there are trays of sand and water that can spill, and little humans that can spill them. They sit in their offices in the first term of a new headship, starting an affair with their computers, and say to the visitor, 'I've got a lot to do here'.

One of their favourite parts of the school is the entrance hall where there's a notice that they see many times every day. It has the school name on it, and their own, with all their qualifications. So 'Cert Ed, BA, MA, PhD, FRSA, OBE, JP' (this is a real example) can remind them, whenever life lets them down, that their rise to the heights they now know is a certainty. It has happened. What is happening now matters little. These headteachers are collectors of baubles. You feel surprised that they haven't put up there on that board their swimming certificates, their scout badges or their driving test.

There are, it is well known, certain truths about life

that will tend to help us not get into trouble. One is, never get involved in any occasion spelt 'Fayre', or named and announced as a 'Funday'. Steer clear of any event that threatens face-painting. Avoid pubs that have 'Smart casual dress only' over the door; also pubs with fat bouncers. Do not rely on casual acquaintances who quote approvingly editorials in the *Daily Mail*. Two other golden rules to add here are: be wary of teachers with lots of letters after their names made public, and also teachers with personalized number plates. These individuals are telling you things that you don't wish to know, and if you know them, it will not help in any way.

Working with the Computer Head

The best of the computer heads are good to work with. This is because they have seen that their job is to enable you to work at your best, and, surprising as it may seem, much of their time at the computer is spent doing this. They are paving your way and knocking down barriers in front of your dearest schemes: finding the help you need from advisers and other Inset suppliers and getting you on courses. One such head I know is, on the face of it, a giveaway – string of letters on the school board, Ford Orion, immaculate suit – but his staff told me that things get done, and that there are sometimes things that he doesn't understand, like courses in subjects other than his own (though it has been many years since he had a subject in the sense of teaching it).

Other computer heads are less enabling. He or she may be tiresome company, but it is not hard to work professionally and creatively in the school. The vacuum for you, if you like any of the subjects you teach, and enjoy the company of children, will be where you should hear encouragement for your work. As this head knows nothing about it, it will not come from the holy of holies in the admin corridor.

On the other hand, you might be moved to experimental, innovative work in the classroom. You may want, for example, as an Anglo-Catholic working with 6 year olds in a church school, to set up an altar with candles in your classroom, or, as a racing enthusiast, a turf accountant's shop, rather than the usual baker's, and you can do it because your head won't recognize it as experimental and innovative even if she sees it; unless, of course, the experiment involves semtex and fertilizer or elephants' dung or a tent with the names of all your lovers felt-tipped round the inside. If you do any of these things, rumours will eventually reach your boss.

With computer heads, it is wise to present a front that is sympathetic to them. It takes a few minutes each week to wise up on the gov-talk that is so precious to this specimen. As I will say in Chapter 5, the *Guardian* on Tuesday, or *The Times Educational Supplement* on Friday well repay the couple of pounds you'll have to lay out to keep in the know.

Mr and Ms Management

Related to the computer head are Mr and Ms Management. I have joyfully collected, over the years, examples of management-speak, both for my own delight and for the delight of my friends in the pub. But it would be a mistake to assume that these idiocies are a trivial matter, a mere joke, because, as George Orwell made clear, the way we use language gives away whether we are honest or dishonest. Look, for example, in my greenhouse at these lurid specimens of the genre.

A local educational authority has an 'officer for quality assurance' and that officer has issued a paper. It says, among other things:

The aim is to create a streamlined service providing a range of customer services [their repeat of 'service'] . . . We shall best attain our best aims of

Maximum delegation

Delayering

Shorter lines of communication

Teaching with a Dodgy Headteacher

Flexibility

By organising our activities into 'business units'

This is funny, but, like all the best funny things, such as *Fawlty Towers*, *The Office* and the Fool in *King Lear*, it is also serious, often deadly so. 'Customer', as many commentators have pointed out, distorts the relationship between teacher and learner, if only because it implies that only the student is a learner. It also implies, dangerously, that learning is a commodity. It makes education a grocer's shop. The banal 'delivery' metaphor speaks of an unpleasant world where teachers have learned everything, and children nothing. So all the teachers have to do is deliver their learning at full volume down a speaking tube.

In James Joyce's *Ulysses*, Mr Deasy suggests to Stephen: 'You were not born to be a teacher, I think?' and Stephen replies: 'A learner rather'. Neither of them realizes that to be a teacher you have to be both. Indeed, all learners are teachers, too. A few minutes' thought reveals to most of us learning we have gained from children: about their minds and the way they work, about the lives they lead, even about subjects which they know more than we do. In this last category, in my experience, come fishing, football, popular culture and, in one startling example, the London Underground.

'Maximum' delegation in the document quoted

earlier is inadvertently honest. It means that the person at the top does nothing at all, and that everyone underneath does everything. 'Delayering' is more obscure than *Finnegans Wake*, as far as I'm concerned. 'Flexibility' on its own, with or without a bullet point, tells us nothing. And 'business units' tells us everything we need to know about this organization: we must be business men and women if we are to succeed. We must be, not in collaboration, but in competition with the school down the road. We must even be, at times, in competition with each other (which class has won the best-behaved cup this week? Or has won the most 'Headteacher says well done!' stickers?).

Private Eye, my constant companion since my grammar school days, provides fortnightly examples of newspeak that is either meaningless, misleading or both. Take this example (*Private Eye*, 21 January – 3 February 2005):

> Sean [headteacher] is a firm believer in the fundamental importance of learning to learn and has introduced radical changes to lesson delivery.
>
> He values heart and mind enhancement of systemic change and emphasises the optimism of self-belief.

Managerialism in education didn't really take hold until the middle 1980s. Then, headteachers were sent free copies of a new magazine devoted to the subject. I wrote about it for *The Times Educational Supplement* (1987), noting that the contributors had no interest in children. 'One writer' (I wrote) 'called for a "progressive movement seeking at least the possibility of choosing full-time provision in a service which meets the needs of . . ." '

'Children' you assume. But no. 'Working parents'. There was not one mention of children in the whole issue. I became certain that the main purpose of management was to distance managers from the messy human reality of the classroom.

Image is critical to this headteacher. One writer told us that 'individual schools must take responsibility for changing the national image of comprehensive schools'. Our logos and letterheads, our school uniforms, are more important than what we do in the classroom. This has been taken to an extreme with the fashion of mottos. When my mother died in St Thomas's Hospital in London, my brother and I noted that, on its name board it said 'Serving the Community'. 'What,' my brother asked dryly, 'what else should they be doing?'

But today, these mottos proliferate. Outside our local further education college it proclaims, alongside a photograph of seven students, one African-Caribbean, one Asian, one in a wheelchair, the whole an exercise in tokenism: 'Excellence through diversity'. Outside a pub a few miles up the road, the motto is 'A more enchanting option'. It is a pity that these two legends couldn't be exchanged.

The management head doesn't distinguish between training and education. This is central to the whole issue of learning. We train each other to ride bikes, to drive cars, to play football, to take the first steps in using a calculator. When, on the other hand, we talk about the free exchange of ideas, intellectual concepts and perspectives, we educate. Training is about ensuring someone goes down a railway track of our own, or, more likely these days, someone else's laying. Education is about love and pain and the whole damn thing.

Management deals in mechanistic clichés. Its keywords are 'enterprise', 'efficiency', 'training', 'input', 'skills' and 'investment'. In contrast, education, being about pushing things further, abhors the cliché, as much as poetry does, and its keywords are 'honesty', 'passion', 'human' and the like. That last group of words would have stood out in the management magazine I reviewed like nuns in a disorderly house.

When one management book came out about a headteacher 'turning a school around' (a phrase to make a teacher's blood run cold), I went first to the index, as you do when you are reviewing a book. There were plenty of references to computers, industry, business education – and only two for the arts. And both of those were concerned with music, which is significant, because music, unlike, for example, poetry can be used to impress, and can easily be part of the image that the headteacher is keen to project on to the local community. Poetry, on the other hand, 'stubbornly still insists upon/being read or ignored' (Auden 1976), and has no place in impressing the mayor or the prospective parliamentary candidate. So no index references for it in this management book.

As I write, the government is talking, after a long silence on the subject (about a quarter of a century), about 'creative teaching'. Successive administrations have been responsible for the drive to make schools the opposite of creative, and there is no apology for their being wrong then if they are right now. And, as Ted Wragg has pointed out (*Guardian* 7/9/04) schools cannot become creative again without 'shak[ing] off the suffocating embrace of nationalisation'. Understandably, 'teachers are too afraid to innovate'. They have been dragooned into a system where taking risks – a prerequisite of innovation and creativity – might land them in trouble.

When I was in my final headship – this was before the days when Ofsted ruled – the local authority announced that the school was to undergo an inspection. We passed, but at the end of it, an adviser told me: 'I suspect that you are using the children to protect yourself from your managerial responsibilities.' That sums up the perversions of management. It's like telling a man playing with his children, 'You're using your family to

How to Teach with a Hangover

protect yourself from your responsibility to drink in the pub'.

All headteachers have to keep a close eye these days on statistics such as SATs results. But some of them, the best, keep these things, despite pressure from advisers, inspectors and politicians, in perspective. Mr and Ms Management, on the other hand, are obsessed with them. In an attempt to face the reality of what testing is like for the children themselves, I wrote this poem:

The SATs

They've been testing the children for a long time.
Outside, summer rain is a silver downpour.
The field sucks it thirstily. Or it bounces

bull's-eyes from the playground. In the classroom
Miss thinks: 'I shouldn't be doing this'
but she has her orders; smiles at Jon and Maxine

who've managed not to cry. Chris and Meldi
finished minutes ago, and gaze at the sodden field
and grey clouds generously pouring drink

on grass and playground. Soon their lives
will be returned to them: a wet lunchtime,
rackety, probably, with trouble. But the dinner ladies

will be kind. 'How did it go, love?'
Jon and Maxine won't think about the SATs
until tonight, when they try to sleep.

Teaching with a Dodgy Headteacher

The Bully

'You didn't really hammer the candidate'

'You've got to tear the candidate apart'

'I want the teachers to be afraid of me. If I give them the toy of democracy it won't work'

'When I appoint a deputy, I know I'll burn him (*sic*) out for two years and then expect him to get a headship'

These are real quotations. It was a training course for headteachers, and I, a headteacher myself, had been asked to submit a fictional application for a job as deputy head. I was interviewed by one group, and their performance was assessed by another group, who had been sitting behind me. Some of the comments by the assessing group are given above. I scribbled them down hurriedly, knowing that they'd come in handy one day. 'Hammer' . . . 'tear apart' . . . 'afraid' . . . 'burn out'. 'The toy of democracy' is wonderfully revealing.

This attitude stemmed from a style of management inspired by Margaret Thatcher, and it may be going out of fashion now. I worked for an education officer who called at a school when the headteacher wasn't there, and changed his diary, because the head had said he couldn't attend a meeting. This officer was famous in the county for 'bouncing' heads around his office if they had displeased him. If there was violence in the schools he managed, he can't have been shocked by it: he began it. Like most violence, it came from the top.

Some violence in schools stems from the headteacher. I watched one head of a special school greeting a boy who was wailing after being dropped off in the minibus. He leaned over him, palms flat against the wall, and shouted louder than the boy wailed, 'We've got a poet in school today, that will be great, don't you understand?' As the poet, I viewed the scene with unmixed feelings.

The Person Headteacher

On the other hand, there are headteachers who are passionate about the children they teach, and what they can teach those children, and what (this is critical) they can learn from those children. While the focal point of the computer head's study is, of course, the gleaming state-of-the-art machine, and the management head's is the targets set him by his elders and betters, and the aggressive head is concerned with getting his or her own way, the person head's study has children's paintings on the walls; and notes from children saying thank you for a story in assembly. In this study, there are toys to play with while parents are being interviewed. I have described a study like this before (Sedgwick 2002):

> . . . there is a large, low square wooden table in the middle. His neat desk, with its computer, is pushed to one wall. Dried plants as tall as me firework out of ceramic pots in two corners of the room. There is an eclectic collection of recent books about teaching . . . the usual statutory files, from central government and from the local authority look neat and undisturbed in one corner . . .

The headteacher of this school teaches regularly and knows every child's name. In another similar school, the head once said to me that he deals with the 'crap' by ignoring it. Over his desk, stuck into the crack between the wall and the notice board, are gleaming CD-ROMs, looking like some modern art installation of low ambitions. 'They're the stuff the authority sends that is no use to me.'

These are the signs of person headteachers. They are around the school. When you see headteacher parking spaces unoccupied, it is not because they are 'working from home'. There are administrative wobbles in the person head's school. She has, typically, booked a string quartet to play to KS2 when the children in Year 5 are swimming. They belong to your union. I think this is probably contentious, but you can learn a lot about headteachers by finding out what union they belong to. The computer head and the management head are almost certainly in the National Association of Head Teachers (NAHT), which isn't a union at all, but a mildly critical advisory body for government and authorities. The person head is probably in the most inclusive union, the National Union of Teachers. He stands with the teachers.

Management is an interesting concept when it is brought to bear on primary education. It ignores anything that is not concerned with money. It tries to disguise this with cant phrases like 'cost-effectiveness', but this doesn't take things very far. Why should something that is cost-effective be necessarily effective for human beings, like children and teachers?

How Should you Deal with the Computer Head and Mr and Ms Management?

Before you take a job, find out as much about a school and its head as you can. Gossip and listen to gossip, but treat what you hear with care. Research: find out from teachers in the school, parents with children in the school and the children themselves, what they think of the place. Do not trust the annual league table. Be ready at interviews to ask questions: How would you sum up the values of this school? Do you exclude children from classrooms, and, if so, where do they go? I am interested in art. Would you fund trips to the National Gallery, and materials to follow up those trips in practical ways? And the like.

When you're there, what should you do?

The computer headteacher will not know much about you. Nor will the managerialist. And those bullies: stand up to them. The person head on the other hand – love him to bits. Put up with her administrative wobbles, and encourage her as much she encourages you. Treat him like an equal, and hug him when he's low, and give her the occasional bottle of Guinness. Do your bit to make sure the staffroom rings with laughter sometimes. You are lucky with this person, and with the pair of you, and the rest of the staff, you can make a school a community where everybody is a learner; where everybody is doing their bit to prise off the clammy hold of management. Be grateful that you haven't got a dodgy headteacher. Be compassionate, because your person head has to endure the most boring meetings.

Interval: A Glimpse into a Headteachers' Meeting

When I was a headteacher, meetings were a problem for me. Whether they were parts of induction courses, or routine meetings about subjects like 'Privatization of Groundstaff', they bored me silly at first, and then came to distress me. Also, it occurred to me that most teachers have no idea what goes on when their headteacher's car park space is empty because the boss is 'at a meeting'. Therefore here is a brief interval about them, by someone who used to be there.

Induction courses for headteachers are barometers of changing views of education. They are not important compared with the orders that governments send to schools, with their ever-changing rules about curriculum and assessment and the rest. They are not important compared to what parents say outside the gates of schools and the versions of what they say that the media print. They are not important compared with what teachers sitting in staffrooms say.

But these strange quasi-masonic gatherings, and what goes on in them, tell us something about the way the wind is blowing. So here are two such meetings, separated by six years in time, but by a great gulf in their ideologies.

One thing all such meetings have in common is a division of types. Keen tyro heads sit near the front, anxious to imprint the images of their eager, polished faces on the chief education officer and his or her deputies. When an officer says 'this may involve some administrative complexity', these heads write in their notebooks 'this may involve some administrative complexity'. The bad lads and lasses sit where the bad lads and lasses in school assemblies have always sat, when they are allowed, in the back row. Here, less polished, and with a frequently satirical bent, they mutter criticisms of the official line, make private jokes and even pass notes.

When I went on my first heads' induction meeting in Hertfordshire in 1975, the subject matter was, on the face of it, the quality of children's work, especially the visual arts. I say, on the face of it. Really it was about how that work should be displayed; how a school could be a 'pleasing' (a key word, this) environment. We were told to encourage the erection of tasteful hessian-covered display screens, of trellises which could divide large

Interval: A glimpse into a Headteachers' Meeting

areas, and the use of large houseplants, and how, with the help of dads, to convert PE equipment storage areas into libraries with pleasant seating. It was about show.

When I went on my second induction meeting, in Suffolk in 1981, there was an item on the agenda of the first meeting: 'Managing the school plant.' I gazed at this uncomprehendingly until I realized it meant 'plant' in the sense of building and environs, not monstera or spider plant or cactus. Other items on that agenda also nonplussed me. 'Cost-effectiveness', 'accountability', 'managing the governors', 'finance meeting' – all this made my blood, if not actually run cold, drop in temperature. It was a long way from the supposed child-centredness of my first heads' course.

The rest of the new agenda was about financial responsibilities. This had been the job of the local education authority during my earlier time as a head, and therefore – or partly therefore – I knew nothing about it. Also, I was frightened of the prospect of managing money, which I have never been good at. I don't manage the money in my pocket very well. Managing a school budget was going to be a frightening and uninteresting challenge. It promised hours of tedium. If there were positive reasons for entering the teaching profession, and there were, not having to manage a budget was one of the most potent negative ones. I knew from the first that I didn't want to be a businessman.

How to Teach with a Hangover

Many agenda items were about legal responsibilities. These frightened me for different reasons. I think I'd assumed that schools got by on a kind of unspoken goodwill, as a friendship or a marriage is supposed to do. Parents and teachers wanted the same things for their children, as friends or married partners wanted the same things for their friends or their partners. They wanted mutual happiness and mutual success. These are unfashionable words now, educationally, when we are told to be concerned with league tables and SATs.

And I think I was right. Most schools had goodwill built into them. Now there appeared, along with the government's strictures, a brown folder, *The Headteacher's Legal Guide*. What sort of a world was this? And how much did mine differ from it? I was frightened. I didn't mind accountability, as long as this meant accountability to the children and their parents. But now we were being made accountable to politicians and bureaucrats who seemed (to judge from the first National Curriculum) to understand nothing about learning and teaching. The new world was also about show because it wasn't concerned with the main issue, what children and teachers did.

In Suffolk, on the second of the induction courses, we were asked to write down our priorities in improving our school. Sitting in the back row with my friend Stuart, I wrote: 'Evaluate and improve the teaching of language.' I would have extended this, given the chance, with

Interval: A glimpse into a Headteachers' Meeting

paragraphs about how teaching anything always involves teaching language; you can't teach art or science, or anything, without being a language teacher. Stuart, who was to experience a unique career progression later – moving from his second headship into scouting for Watford Football Club, and moving then to the management of Wimbledon FC, later Milton Keynes Dons – wrote something similar about the importance of PE and games. How he would have justified this I don't know, but I would have trusted him. He was concerned with people and their understanding of themselves and their world, and the relationship between those people and their world. He was an educationalist.

But another head, turning round from his place in the front row, read his statement aloud, and here I saw the way the world was going: 'Check on the state of the school's infrastructure.' 'Infrastructure!' Stuart and I laughed at him rudely and openly over pints in The Spreadeagle at lunchtime. But he had got the right answer. Later, at home, I looked the word up in a dictionary, and couldn't find it. Eventually I located it in Longmans: 'an underlying foundation or basic framework . . . the permanent installations required for military purposes.' I found that last clause disturbing. Like 'objectives', all the current managerial terminology came from the American military.

Somebody from County Hall told us, 'You are the chief education officer's middle managers, and you'd better believe it'. The men and women in the front row glowed with quiet pride. As a member of both the back row and the National Union of Teachers, I saw myself alongside my staff, rather than above them. If it came to management, all of my teachers would be managers of the school in different situations: one organizing in-service education to prepare for the new curriculum idea, one organizing meetings for new parents, and so on.

The only useful idea I remember was a distinction between what was 'urgent' and what was 'important'. This book is about issues I deem important: the very nature of education; love and its problems; what a headteacher should be like; cynicism; inspectors; and behaviour. The heads' meetings were concerned with neither the urgent nor the important, but with making the world bright for politicians and managers.

4 'The kids round here'

When will the bell ring, and end this weariness?

D. H. Lawrence

There are few better ways of getting the feel of an earlier age than to read its fiction. In this chapter, I will look at cynicism in schools as seen, in part, in novels by Dickens and Charlotte Brontë, and then make links between these books and teaching today. But not only does fiction teach us about the past. It is also a way of preparing us for our joys and sorrows. In other words, it teaches us about our own futures. We can see this most clearly in children's fiction, where a book like Maurice Sendak's *Where the Wild Things Are* prepares the child for those times of rejection, and reconciliation, that family life inevitably entails.

Charity (meaning, as I've said before, love) believeth all things. Cynicism, in contrast, believeth nothing. It is often expressed in the staffroom by remarks like (following a recounting of a child's anecdote) 'Oh well, he would say that'. Cynicism is resolutely cagey and unimpressed by shows of openness. It distrusts. You can't fool me, the speaker implicitly says. It takes pride in not believing things, including things visiting writers say. Their aim is to help every child produce a truthful first draft by the end of the day. But, says the cynical teacher, 'You won't get any decent work from the kids round here'.

Cynicism is also expressed in casual cruelty: 'Make her learn a page of her reading book, she'll hate it.' It is also expressed by insulting stereotyping. Books about education rarely give air to this, but teachers sometimes refer to 'dimmos' and 'herberts' and the like. When hearing these things, step away from them, and, as the motto of the University of East Anglia has it, 'Do different'. How would I feel if I knew that every remark of mine was greeted with (in my absence) 'Well, he would say that'; or if others said about me 'Give him that to do, he'll hate it'; or if I were referred to as a 'thickie'?

Patrick Whittaker (in Lang 1988) quotes Carl Rogers' summary of a view of education that is essentially cynical. To summarize, pupils cannot be expected to learn, and when they do, they learn only (or merely) what the teacher teaches. And that learning is nothing more than an accumulation of facts and figures. And, moreover, the pupils are not active learners, but objects to be manipulated, jugs to be filled. Contrast that with this wonderful truth, expressed by John Holt in the same article:

> Almost every child, on the first day he sets foot in a school building, is smarter, more curious, less afraid of what he doesn't know, better at finding and figuring things out, more confident, resourceful, persistent and independent, than he will ever again be in his schooling.

A question hangs in the air: if this is true (and my observation of young children in school suggests that it is), what are schools doing to spoil this amazing potential, to take away curiosity and to instil fear of the unknown? A girl was blessed with artist parents, and had been looking at and drawing trees in every season from a young age. When she came home from her first day at school, she produced a drawing she'd done, a lollipop tree. 'Why have you drawn a tree like that?' her mother asked. 'You know what trees look like'. 'That's the way we draw trees in school,' the girl replied. 'The fool sees not the same tree that the wise man sees,' as Blake tells us ('Proverbs of Hell' in Blake 1958). The school, in a single day, had taken the child's curiosity and knowledge and replaced it with a stereotype. The cynicism of this act was no less appalling because it was unconscious.

How to Teach with a Hangover

Cynicism in the Judaeo-Christian West derives, in part, from the doctrine of original sin. Because we are, according to this doctrine, conceived in iniquity, every subsequent act, from our yelling for food and comfort, through our attempted escapes as toddlers from our parents' control, to our first sexual moves, can be interpreted in a low way: a cynical way.

Adults' annoyance at the excesses of children and adolescents is rooted in jealousy. Adults are cynical about the behaviour of the young because they have neither the energy nor the freedom to behave like their children. They remember playing in mud with spade and bucket, if only sub- or half-consciously, but they cannot, or may not, do it now. Watching that child walk up the garden steps caked in earth, or watching her swishing, with intent eyes, a little net around a rock pool, they are reproached by their half-remembered past. And often, those parents weren't allowed, when they were children, to wallow and play. Their childhoods were more imprisoned. Mud wasn't good. Dirt was bad.

Then, of course, they see their teenagers out of the front door to go clubbing and drinking, and, as they look forward to an early night of passion, cocoa coursing through their veins, they remember the din of their own youth, and it sounds muted. Members of the older generation, unless they are vigilant, become cynical. Why wasn't life like that for us? Where has our energy gone?

But though original sin, which is in part a fear of the

body and its energies, is the root of cynicism, there is a truth in this doctrine. Humanity's potential for wickedness glowers from the pages of every newspaper, every television screen. And we can see it in children, as well. Looking at innocent faces singing in an assembly, or working on a piece of art, or dancing in a gym, it is easy to forget their occasional casual cruelty. Then a news story is splashed in the paper, or on television. Fifty girls in an all girls' school surround one girl who has kissed one of the mob's ex. They taunt and hit and kick. And we remember original sin again.

When I was a headteacher, I glimpsed a relationship between sentimentality and viciousness. Often it was the 10-year-old child with the fondness for her teddies who could lead a vendetta against another child who had been deemed unfit for membership of the gang. In adults, the most sentimental are those who are not good at feelings. When those feelings, such as they are, are thwarted, those adults become vicious. They become stalkers or bullies. They proclaim their love loudly and in horrible ways, while acting with what looks more like hatred. Sometimes, as Oscar Wilde says, they kill the thing they love.

But in the classroom, notwithstanding original sin, we have to believe in a certain moral freshness. Nearly all children are vulnerable in their dealings with adults. Given the chance, they express, unselfconsciously, their innermost fears and wishes, in a way that most adults find almost impossible. A child wrote in a letter to Father Christmas (the class had been asked to write letters on behalf of someone else), 'Please give my grandma rest because she has cancer'. In Causley's poem 'School at four o'clock', the children come to school 'hungry and innocent', and the cynics are the teachers. With the final phrase of the poem, 'And were not fed', Causley directs us to Milton's 'Lycidas', and those whose

> . . . lean and flashy songs
> Grate on their scrannel pipes of wretched straw;
> The hungry sheep look up, and are not fed . . .

Here 'scrannel' means thin, lean, meagre, and is a perfect word for a cynical government's legislation, or a cynical teacher's teaching. 'I've always found chalk-and-talk was good enough, and I won't change.' 'Because it works' is a phrase used to justify a cynical attitude: 'we use the Ladybird scheme here because it works' a head said to me 30 years ago. Thin, lean, meagre; I doubt whether even the publishers of the Peter and Jane books would dispute that description.

There have always been cynics in the profession, 'dog-like, churlish, disposed to rail or find fault, disposed to sneer at the sincerity or goodness of human motives and actions' (SOED – the word stems from the Greek for dog). That is certainly true if (as I am) we are to believe the novelists. There has always been cruelty, with its infliction of pain by the strong on the weak, railing as it does on the innocence of others, is surely the most extreme form of cynicism.

Learning from the Novels

In *Jane Eyre*, Lowood School is where 'Jane . . . seems to have spent more time thinking about her frozen limbs and her empty stomach than in learning the lessons of the scriptures'. In Juliet Barker's biography of the Brontë family, it is clear that the real life equivalent of Lowood was probably just as bad. Run by evangelical clergymen, the food was mostly inedible. Punishments ranged from learning portions of scripture to whipping, and frequently girls died. These included the Brontë writers' elder sisters. The cynicism here isn't only in the events *per se*, but in the fact that they stem from devout religious conviction.

If our bodies are essentially sinful, it is wrong to cosset them; a true Christian faith (it was argued) will come from privation. In any case, there is a second reason why the body hardly matters: it is a temporary convenience, necessary, but no more than that, for our journey through this world to the next, which could appear at any time. All the poor virgins at Lowood School had to do was to make sure that their lamps were trimmed, ready for the arrival of the bridegroom and the heavenly kingdom. They did not need to be well fed. 'This world is not my home . . . I'm just a-passing through' as the country and western song has it. Every Sunday morning represents a week's march nearer home.

A Modern Fundamentalist Cynicism

Fundamentalist Christianity is guilty of similar cynicism today. With a relatively small financial input, private benefactors are able to buy into secondary education. Their schools are called academies, and the fee expected of the benefactors is £2 million. The taxpayer's contribution, on the other hand, is £20 million, with annual payments of around £5 million (for details, see John Harris, 15 January 2005). Despite this imbalance, the benefactors are licensed to ignore the National Curriculum and to appoint most of the governors in these schools. This, of course, gives them extraordinary power over, first, what is taught in the school, second, how it is taught, and third, how the school is managed. Thus they gain power over children's minds.

For example, the Vardy Foundation is in the process of opening schools. Because Sir Reg Vardy, a millionaire car dealer, is a fundamentalist Christian, these schools will teach the literal interpretation of the Genesis story of

creation alongside evolution. Presumably, a literal interpretation of that verse about rich men, the eye of a nee-
dle and getting into the Kingdom of Heaven is not
encouraged, but fundamentalists are always selective in
the verses they choose to emphasize. Both creationism
and evolutionism, the foundation says, ignoring the fact
that there is evidence for evolution and none for creationism, are 'faith positions'. In other words, they will
attempt to persuade children that the world was created
in six days; that the first chapter of Genesis, and the first
few verses of the second chapter, are to be seen as history, when in fact they are Hebrew liturgy. The fact that
the rest of the verses in Genesis 2 tell a different story
matters little to them.

The Vardy Foundation believes also that homosexuality is a sin. The educational adviser to the Foundation,
John Burn, and Nigel McQuoid, principal at one of the
schools, have written:

> If relativist philosophy is acceptable, then sado-
> masochism, bestiality and self-abuse are to be con-
> sidered as wholesome activities . . . the Bible says
> clearly that homosexual activity is against God's
> design. I would indicate that to young folk.

The cynicism in yoking sadomasochism and bestiality on
the one hand, with self-abuse and homosexuality on the
other is breathtaking, and so is the expressed belief that

homosexuality is 'against God's design'. Many Biblical scholars would suggest that the issue is nothing like that simple: see, for example, Jeffrey John's book (1993) which reiterates points made many times before; first that the sin of Sodom was not homosexuality, but lack of hospitality; and that the other Bible texts need to be seen in the context of their times.

The Vardy Foundation has, very cheaply, bought an influence on the minds of young people. Also, academies, unlike state schools, are not liable to be fined for excluding pupils, and the exclusion rate at the Vardy school in Middlesbrough, the *Guardian* reports, is ten times the national average. This suggests that the foundation is less tolerant of dissent than it should be; a school's job is to cope with bad behaviour, not to expel those responsible for it. And these disaffected pupils end up at the local comprehensive, thus exacerbating the differences in the schools' intake, and making it easier for both to demonize what a government cynically called 'bog standard comprehensives', and to lionize the academies.

The government says that academies provide choice. But an administration's duty is not to provide choice but to provide a consistent service throughout the country. Cynically, the government allows schools to become specialists in sport, or science, or modern languages, when the students require (to use an outdated phrase that was all the rage a few years ago) a broad and balanced curriculum; a curriculum that offers a decent education in all the subjects.

Back to the Novels

Dickens provides probably the most famous example of the cynical teacher in *Nicholas Nickleby*, with his one-eyed Wackford Squeers ('the popular prejudice', of course, 'runs in favour of two') who saw the boys entirely in terms of the money they brought in: 'I took down ten boys; ten twentys – two hundred pound'. This contrasted with his advertisement:

> Youth are boarded, clothed, booked, furnished with pocket-money, provided with all necessaries, instructed with all languages living or dead, mathematics, orthography, geometry, astronomy, trigonometry, the use of the globes, algebra, single stick (if required), writing, arithmetic, fortification, and every other branch of classical literature. Terms, twenty guineas per annum. No extras, no vacations, and diet unparalleled.

Apart from the gargantuan dishonesty of this account, there is a deeper cynicism in that little phrase 'no vacations': the parents of the unfortunates at Dotheboys

How to Teach with a Hangover

School (Squeers' school) never wanted to see their off-spring again, and Mr Squeers, with this little phrase, says they won't have to.

If you say I am dwelling pointlessly on the past, I have to say that I was reminded of Mr Squeers when I visited a new playschool in 2001. 'And here,' said the proprietor, and ex-state school headteacher, two-eyed physically, as far as I can remember, but one-eyed in her motivation, much like the fundamentalist Christians running the academies, 'is where my money-spinners will go – the babies'. Her advertisement was fulsome, too, like Squeers'. The increasing need for provision for very young children, so that their mothers can go out to work, yields money for the many playgroups springing up with their patronizing names: Tinytots, Little Shoots, and the like.

Dickens, of course, had suffered at the hands of the teaching profession. Mr Creakle's words to the boys in the autobiographical *David Copperfield* smell of the chalk and cruelty of schools at that time, and of their emotional and physical coldness: 'Now, boy, this is a new half. Take care what you're about . . . Come fresh up to the lessons, I advise you, for I come fresh up to the punishment. I won't flinch. It will be no use rubbing yourselves: you won't rub the marks out that I shall give you.' The marks on children's spirits made by SATs won't be easily rubbed away, either.

The most famous educational passage in Dickens is

the opening of *Hard Times*. Mr Grandgrind displays a subtler form of cynicism than the one I have defined above, but it is cynicism nonetheless: in the face of the evidence, like modern politicians relying on testing, he insists that all that matters in life are

Facts. Teach these boys and girls facts and nothing but Facts. Facts alone are wanted in life . . . Stick to Facts, sir!

This obsession, and its poignant effect, is seen in the next chapter, when the girl, Cissy Jupe, who has known and tended horses since her babyhood, and who is intimate with their look, sound, smell and feel, cannot define one. But Bitzer – the sun '[appears] to draw out of him whatever colour he ever possessed' – can:

'Bitzer,' said Thomas Grandgrind. 'Your definition of a horse'. 'Quadruped. Graminivorous. Forty teeth, namely twenty-four grinders, four eye-teeth, and twelve incisors. Sheds coat in spring; in marshy countries, sheds hoofs, too. Hoofs hard, but requiring to be shod with iron. Age known by marks in mouth'.

Bitzer can parrot all this without knowing anything about horses. In the same way, a modern child can define a phoneme without knowingly using one, or

91

without having her writing or speech extended or enriched one whit. We have to get beyond the numbers game, beyond mere facts, beyond 'quadruped' and 'graminivorous', to the smell of a horse in its stable, its sweat on its flanks, the soft munch as it eats. We have to recognize Cissy's, rather than Bitzer's, as the true learning, and find ways to evaluate it. Evaluating Bitzer's learning is easy and meaningless and, as Blake says, hitting the nail on the head as he does so often, measurement is for the year of dearth, the mean times, the times of the lean cattle.

The current government's obsession with facts, and with collections of targets, is part of the same shabby materialism that ignores what human beings are like. As John White (1990) writes,

> Thought about education ... should begin with the articulated, complex picture of personal well-being ... and not with the flattened-out, uni-dimensional account of the utilitarians and economists.

Also, these targets, if we examine the implicit metaphor, focus on what the child will be rather than on what he or she is now.

But we can go back farther than Grandgrind's cynicism. Michael Rosen's anthology *The Penguin Book of Childhood* (1994) is as eloquent a document as I have read about the treatment of children by teachers. The front cover of the hardback edition is a painting by Jan Steen, 'The Village School'. Steen's dates are 1626–1679, and he was Dutch. I mention these facts so that you can visualize the clothes his characters are wearing, all natural beiges and fawns, Hessian clothes.

The picture is in the National Gallery of Ireland in Dublin. Crowded round a small table are seven figures: a schoolmaster holding what looks like a wooden spoon – it is probably a pandy bat, a stick kept for the sole purpose of hitting children – over the half-open palm of a mop-haired boy, who is wiping a tear away from his eye as he waits for the next blow. A girl, caught in the middle of the composition, her face highly lit, looks on in mixed fascination and horror. That will happen to me soon, she is thinking, if I'm not careful. A hatted figure is absorbed in a book, while other children take less interest in the proceedings than the girl: looking away, as if this is to be expected (which, of course, it was) or glancing up from a sheet of paper.

Cynicism and Common Sense

All this should alert us to the possibilities of cynicism that common sense, routinely considered a Good Thing, generates. It was obviously common sense to hit children until quite recently – it was still allowed when I started teaching in the late 1960s. The art master at my London grammar school was responsible for corporal punishment – isn't that a blood-curdling sentence? – but he had a cane rather than a pandy bat. To someone, it was common sense for the art master to be responsible for the cane. It was common sense to put dunce caps on children in Victorian times, and to punish girls at the school the Brontë sisters attended by making them memorize parts of the Bible, in the belief that this would make them better Christians. In our times, common sense is an excuse for not thinking, for not innovating, for not working out how we might do something better. Its allied term is 'it works', usually applied to some dreary reading book that is like a book only in the limited senses that it has printing in it and it is bound. Books like this are what Victorian scholars called *biblia abiblia*, books that are not books.

It is common sense that the teaching of grammar is an indispensable condition of improvement in children's writing. Indeed, a right-wing newspaper is hardly ready for press without a why-oh-why article on children's failures to identify verbs and nouns. But a research study at the University of York in 2004 shows that there is no evidence that grammar teaching has any beneficial effect on children's writing. As Philip Pullman, writing in the *Guardian*, 22 January 2005, says, 'common sense seems to have been routed by the facts. If we want children to write well, giving them formal instruction in grammar turns out not to be any use; getting them actually writing seems to help a great deal more'.

As Pullman goes on to say, the common sense brigade often talks about 'the basics' in writing. But spelling, grammar and punctuation, for real writers, are not basics at all, but matters to be dealt with late in the composition of an article, a story or a poem. When I first drafted this book, I was intent on getting the right words to express what I felt and believed. Now, as I write the last draft, I watch out for grammatical problems, and I improve (I hope) my punctuation. Later, when I read proofs, I will correct minor infelicities of expression. They are minor matters. This, on the other hand, is basic: the writer's use of language to understand him or herself, the world, and the language itself, and, through that understanding, to tell the truth.

The second entry in Rosen's anthology comes from the New Kingdom of Ancient Egypt (2000–1500 BC). A child speaks to us about his experience of school from, maybe, 4,000 years ago: 'I grew up beside you, you smote my back, and so your teaching entered my ear.' Cynics today do not smite knowledge into children: that would be illegal. Instead, they drive it in with the force of their wills, backed up by attainment targets and the school's position in the league tables, and its reputation with Ofsted. Because the ancient Egyptian teacher's relationship with his pupil was personal, it was probably preferable to the effects of this dreary machinery.

Cynical Teachers Today

Cynical teachers cannot get away with as much as old timeservers did. We live in a litigious society, where a step out of place into political areas, a dubious sexual relationship, or violence, will land us in the courts. But I did work in a public school where the headmaster suggested the resurrection of the fag system, because 'bullying wasn't necessarily a bad thing'. He was cried down by his more liberal colleagues. And two teachers from primary schools stick in my mind. One routinely tears up work deemed unsatisfactory.

Another, a deputy head, watches me working with her class as they start writing. She says, 'but they haven't written the title, date and learning objective'. The title, date and learning objective . . .? Over the heads of the children, nervously, I argue with her. Writers don't write their title, date and learning objective first . . . They haven't a clue what their learning objective is . . . They would never think, of such a thing . . . Imagine Graham Greene thinking about what he is aiming at . . . You learn as you write . . . That isn't how writers work.

I'd stumble a bit. She doesn't stumble. She says: 'but

this is a school'. Later, I see that all the children had written the initials 'LO' over every previous piece of work.

That is cynical, even though the teacher didn't know it. It is kowtowing to politicians and their silly requirements. As objectives focus the teacher's attention, not on the child as he or she is now, but as he or she will be when he or she has jumped the next hurdle; they limit learning, because at its most important, it is impossible to imprison inside such a limited concept.

There are indeed cynical teachers, and they will trip up a teacher who still has the light of science in his or her eyes. Some would argue that cynicism is understandable and even to be applauded in times when legislation seems designed to provoke it. But that is to confuse it with scepticism, a different matter. It is right and proper (and our bounden duty) to be sceptical when a government minister tells us to do more about Making British Sport Great Again, when his or her government has been selling off playing fields to developers, or when he or she bangs on about choice when what he or she means is choice for those who can afford it. In these cases, it is the minister who is being cynical, and teachers who have a duty to be sceptical.

Watch and listen to the cynical teachers. They talk about the children 'round here'. I have heard this in all kinds of schools: a private school, for example, where a teacher told me: 'they have all they need materially, but as far as spiritual values are concerned, these children are deprived . . .' This kind of comment is even more common in schools on what are called sink estates.

This is untrue. Gordon Wells (1986), in his research on a Bristol estate, showed that children came into school with far more language than their teachers believed, and that much schooling in the early years was anti-educational. It isn't just lollipop trees. They come with language, and we take it away.

Rejoice in being alone with your class! It is not difficult, if you like them. If you believe, as I do, that, notwithstanding the doctrine of original sin, nearly all children are nearly always good.

If you want to see cynicism rampant, look no further than the next chapter, where we see an organization that wouldn't trust a child to learn or a school to improve; that sees all learning not only as coming exclusively from the teacher, but also as measurable in the most banal sense – with mental ruler; that uses 'mind-forg'd manacles'; that treats the whole shooting match – child, teacher, learning assistant – as a machine made up of objects to be manipulated.

5 Teaching with Ofsted Present

Bring out number, weight & measure in a year of dearth.

Blake, 'Proverbs of Hell'

The child's mind, the child's heart. How can anyone presume to measure what goes on in either?
Emily Roeves, unpublished PhD thesis

Some things are difficult to define. Two spring to mind, prepositions and love. You know them when you come across them. That little nudge, or that growing warmth, will change the direction of a sentence, or a life. Education is also difficult to define, and those who would try to do so with certainty inevitably reveal their thinking as crass.

Often, it is only years after that we understand that we have learnt something, and it will often be a chance occurrence: a teacher's remark, a sentence in our current reading that connected with a sentence we read days, weeks, months, years earlier. Definite, definition: the words reveal an unwarranted certainty about something that can be, and usually is, elusive and surprising. Definable or not, education and learning are immeasurable. The main argument against statistical assessment in schools, whether of the schools themselves, of the teachers, or of the children, is that it is always an attempt to measure what can't be measured. It is important to say at the outset of this chapter that this doesn't mean I don't believe in evaluating what schools are doing.

Researching Your Own Classroom

There are two related methods of evaluating your own teaching. One is to watch carefully what you are doing, and the other is to research it methodically. To be aware of these activities, and to practise them, is to be one step ahead of any Ofsted team, because these methods of judging are based on human reality, rather than dubious dry statistics, which are, notoriously, worse than damn'd lies. Indeed, it's hard to disagree with Burgess (2002) when he says that 'without the bullying tactics of its first chief inspector, Ofsted is revealed as having no thought-out principles or worked out practice of inspection'. He also writes that Ofsted's reports are like 'station announcements, intrusive, vaguely menacing and unintelligible'. His first comment is borne out by a story in the *Guardian* (4 February 2005) which says that the chief inspector overruled his colleagues' findings in order to fail a school which they believed had passed.

The first humane method of judging your work is to look carefully at, and listen carefully to, the processes through which you and the children are going in your classroom. Rather than relying solely on statistics, test results and the like, ask yourself, what is happening here? And is it good? Drop the statutory manacles for a moment, and use the senses of hearing and sight, and try to understand. For example, tape yourself teaching. Play the tape back, and find out much you talked, and how much the children talked. I'll bet the royalties on my last book (I've never been much of a risk-taker) that you, the expert, talked more than the children, the ones who are supposed to be learning how to talk fluently and logically. You will unwittingly have confirmed the truth of the rule of two thirds, which states that two thirds of the time in a given classroom, someone is talking; and that two thirds of that time, it is the teacher, not the children. (I'd go further, and bet that most of that teacher-talk is administrative and disciplinary in character, rather than educational.)

Pay attention to what the children are doing, and, as Simone Weil writes, a light that is in exact proportion to that attention will shine on your (and their) path. You will, to change the metaphor, reap the rewards of that attention in your practice.

You can extend this further. Because your opinion of your classroom practice, however sincere it may be, is biased massively and inevitably in your favour, persuade someone, a parent or a teaching assistant, to watch your work. They are biased too – there is no such thing as balanced reporting, not in journalism, not in research, because we all as observers bring our own baggage to the setting we're observing – but their bias will tend to correct your own. And, as an inspector has pointed out to me, Ofsted personnel have their own baggage too, however much they talk about objectivity.

For example, that parent or that teaching assistant could watch a PE lesson, with a checklist of your questions: Did all the children take a full part in the lesson? Did things happen that you missed? Which children showed physical courage, which showed timidity? Bearing in mind research that suggests that children should get their heartbeats up to 130 or thereabouts at least once a day, and that they rarely achieve this, was there evidence of this happening here? Who got the most/ least out of the lesson? Was your use of language clear? Given that PE lessons, like all lessons, are about language, what opportunities did you give the children to express themselves in speech?

When the children write, see whether they are writing

from inside themselves, about their own concerns, or whether they are writing in a framework imposed on them by entirely adult concerns. Are they playing with what matters to them, or are they trapped in the dull grid of the literacy strategy? And don't rely on your own perspective, but ask that assistant to say what her or she sees.

These analyses of process lead into the second, and even more powerful way, of evaluating your classroom: research. You've begun this already, by just looking and listening, and thereby gaining another perspective on your classroom. But you can extend and strengthen this looking and listening by making it methodical; by changing it into action research, and by making it collaborative.

Work together with other teachers. If you have an informal team constantly looking carefully at, and making notes about, your teaching, you will understand far more clearly what is going on in your (and their) classroom. You are probably friends with at least some of your colleagues. Give these friendships a professional dimension. With the knowledge you will gain from discussions, you can get your retaliation in first with Ofsted when they come. Tell them about this ongoing research project, and what you have found out through it.

History seems to have overtaken the classroom research movement which I studied for an MA 20 years ago. There simply isn't the time to do what I did, as a

How to Teach with a Hangover

headteacher, in one school: arrange time off for teachers so that they could talk about their work. We formed groups to change practice, on the grounds that we would have little respect for a doctor who didn't frequently meet colleagues to see if there were better ways to do things than were currently being used. The school hummed at one point with discussion, especially about how children came to school already emerging as writers, artists and scientists. Now, there isn't the time for this, and also so much of the curriculum is prescribed anyway by Whitehall.

But a new government initiative, Workforce Reform, will give teachers half a day a week to plan, and this should be hijacked by them for research into practice. It may be intended as a vehicle for making teachers obey orders, but, like all such vehicles, it can be subverted. It can be used to enable teachers to grab back some of the ownership of the things they teach, to rebel against their current status as hired hands in the service of a cynical and statistic-obsessed government.

Teachers often say to me plaintively after I have taught their class a lesson in which they have written poems inspired by Shakespeare, Christina Rossetti or Thomas Hood (to name but three), 'I wish we had time for this sort of thing'. Meeting in groups might teach teachers the importance of such writing, especially in the shadow of phonemes and rime, and all the other statutorily-backed trivia.

Dealing with Ofsted

It would be difficult to write about experiences of Ofsted without sounding negative. And I am going to sound pretty negative. But there are ways of countering Ofsted's guns. You can muffle them, or evade them, or even, at times, spike them. The main thing is to know what they are doing. It may look and feel as though they are terrorizing you, or patronizing you. But what they are doing is, to borrow from Geoffrey Hill's translation of Ibsen's play *Brand*, trying 'to measure the measureless'. To inspect a school with a view to putting its practice into categories is to fly in the face of what education is; indeed, it is to fly in the face of what humanity is, much as Bitzer's definition of a horse flies in the face of what a horse is. It is to make a tidy heap of the inherently untidy. It inevitably reduces the significance of education, because only the less important aspects of education are measurable anyway. Can you measure a child's progress in his thinking, in her understanding of the novels of Philip Pullman, in his ability to pray? To pretend you can is to reduce education to the level of 'thinking skills', 'literacy skills' and 'prayer skills' (Level One: 'Places hands accurately together'.)

An Ofsted inspector is like a man who has lost his wedding ring under a tree at night. His friend finds him searching under a nearby lamppost. 'But you didn't lose

How to Teach with a Hangover

it here,' his friend says. 'No,' says the man, 'but at least there is light here'. Sure, there is light where the inspectors search. But the learning is elsewhere, where it is mighty difficult to see, let alone inspect.

It is important to understand this inherent futility, and to be aware of your own strengths. Many teachers are young, and almost all are younger than the inspectors, who are, as one such inspector rather depressingly said to me, 'at the death end of 50'. This means that teachers are more agile mentally. They tend to forget this, because they are so harassed by jacks-in-office dropping rubbish on them from their little height.

If you are attractive (if you are reading this book, you are), with a personality that appeals to children, your day-to-day life in the classroom is humane and kind. You instinctively understand children, what makes them laugh, for example, and your training means you know how to quell a noise, or rebuke a tactless or rude remark. Your sense of humour, your raised eyebrow, your glare, have all served you well in the classroom. When the inspectors come, that rapport will show up to a blind man, and even to an inspector. Hold on to that. Whatever happens, don't let the camaraderie that the children have become accustomed to slip away. First, it will impress anyone; second, it will let the children know that, stressed as the situation might be, it is still normal in some ways.

You are more up-to-date. First, you are in touch with

the children's concerns – their music, their sport and their television. Perhaps (only perhaps) more important, you have found time among all your preparation to look through either *Education Guardian* on Tuesday or *The Times Educational Supplement* over a weekend. Even little journals like the NUT's *Teacher* can offer information about acronyms and the like you can drop into conversation. The *Teacher* is a thin kipper that takes about 10 minutes to fillet.

More substantially, Ted Wragg offers every week in the *Guardian* a view from the liberal, humane left of current government thinking, and sends me into school on some Tuesdays transformed from a depressed and defeated hack into a knight with something rather better to do than count the beans the government thinks so important. Recently, for example, he exposed the absurdities of specialist secondary schools, and the lies told by government about the supposed failure to make students computer literate. John Clare in the *Telegraph* (you read that paper, no doubt, 'for the sport') gives you a view of what the middle classes are thinking, those people who either send their children to private schools, or would like to. Some of these children are, quite likely, in your class.

You know things that the inspectors don't know. One young teacher said to an inspector she had been influenced by the marvellous work she'd seen on courses about Reggio Emilia, a part of Italy with imaginative and

innovative thoughts and practices in early years education. The inspector said 'Reggio Emilia . . ., yes, I've
heard of him, but I haven't read his books . . .' Without
being triumphalist, you should rejoice in and build on
these moments. They are rays of sunlight on your path
through a sometimes gloomy world.

You can baffle inspectors. Pull out a lesson that
doesn't fit with the National Curriculum, but which sat-
isfies elements of it. Prepare to defend it. In one school, I
asked the 6 year olds to 'think of questions that they'd
love to know the answer to, but they don't think they
ever will'. I ask them to cover their eyes and reflect for a
minute or two. Of course, they dart their hands into the
air, that useless practice that survives every educational
change. I say, 'When you've thought of one question,
think of another . . . and another'. They put their hands
down, and think. It is a startling and little recognized fact
that children are offered little opportunity for serious
reflection on a problem. When they do have this chance,
they came up with wonderful things. Here are some I
have lovingly garnered:

♦ Dos god bleeve in me (That was how it was written
   by this 6 year old. Would you correct it?)

♦ How can I tell if a man is evil or not?

♦ My grandfather wasn't a Catholic. Will he get to
   Heaven?

- Why should I pray to God, when he doesn't pray to me?

- Why do my mum and dad shout at each other?

- Why did my mum leave us?

- When will I die?

- Do cats dream?

- Why do adults have power over children when children do not have power over grown-ups?

- How do you get to Heaven?

- Why do teenagers get spots?

- How does the sea suck you away?

- How was the first man born when there was no-one to have a baby?

And I have many others like them. The teachers in one school typed their children's questions up in a large type-face, and put a label on the wall: 'We have been asking philosophical questions.' I had explained to the children the word: 'philo' = love, or friend; 'sophy' = wisdom, or knowledge.

The hapless inspector in this school had trouble working this out. I watched him gazing at the display. What level were these children on? What attainment target were they meeting? What was going on? And yet the whole lesson, which is about philosophy, philology, religion, ethics, Personal, Social and Moral Education, as well as language, is also a literacy hour.

You should challenge judgements. If a lesson is deemed 'good', why wasn't it 'very good'? If 'very good', why not 'excellent'? My Ofsted correspondent assures me that 'the nature of a good lesson is that it has nothing much wrong with it'. There are delicate boundaries between these categories that are worth exploring.

My Ofsted correspondent also tells me that 'appearance' is critical. Throw off the usual dark blues and greys that you wear because of the risk of being spattered with paint for the days of the inspection, and impress with colour and style. It is a matter of morale. And looking better than an inspector can't be difficult.

One Inspector (satisfactory)

Although my friend looks a little frightening the first time you meet him, he is a kind man. He cries easily when moved by art. He runs a small primary school with an unfashionable, almost rebellious passion for those parts of the curriculum that testing cannot reach, the arts. He takes groups of children every year to the Sainsbury Centre at the University of East Anglia, which is a collection of works by, among others, Francis Bacon, Giacometti and Henry Moore, and other giants of the twentieth century.

There are also hundreds of works by lesser-known artists, like the sculptor John Davies, who depicts sad life-size working men in an extremely figurative way, but with one oddity, a large fruit balanced on the head perhaps, or a theatrical mask covering the eyes. There are also hundreds of examples of ancient art, from North America, India and Polynesia. The whole collection was built by Sir Robert and Lady Sainsbury, and it betrays an obsession with the human head. It is housed dramatically in a silver modernist building by Norman Foster, a building both functional and beautiful.

My friend's schoolchildren love the place. They travel round it, and they talk without embarrassment (unusual at that age) about nudes. They are knowledgeable about, and receptive to, the strange and the exotic in a way few adults are. After all, they have only recently arrived from the ultimately strange and the exotic, Heaven. My friend is building on that closeness to God, and hanging on to his own.

At a time when other headteachers were ordering filing cabinets for every classroom, to keep those precious test results in, those statements of special needs, those league tables, those assessment forms, my friend commissioned a stained glass window for the school. Placed in an inner wall between two classrooms for the sake of its safety, it is made of images and colours from the local reservoir: grebes, water, a deep royal blue, various greens for the reeds.

The gap between the purchase of those cabinets and the purchase of that window is emblematic for me. I reflect how the censors' reports on the great Russian poet Pushkin, that seemed so important to the Tsar at the time, have long since rotted, as the content of those cabinets will rot, while the poet's work survives in most of the great languages of the world as that window will survive.

And then this headteacher gave his friends, especially me, a shock. He trained as an Ofsted inspector. I tried to see him in the ranks of suited robots crowding round the flasks of stale coffee on the training course, but I could imagine none of it. How, for example, was he going to coarsen his perception of schools and what goes on in them to 'satisfactory' and 'less than satisfactory', to 'in need of special measures' and 'with serious weak-nesses'? He had always judged his own school by the quality of the processes children were going through. Now it would all be outcomes. In any case, he has always been unwilling to deprecate anyone willingly. How could someone who is unable to make judgements, even about terrorists and Tories, make trite ones about teachers?

The trigger for this decision, he told me, had been an inspection in his own school. An enlightened team gave his school 'a rave review'. My friend said to me, 'They can't be all bad. I know what you think about Ofsted, but this lot really appreciated what we were trying to do'. Also, I suspect, as a creative human being, he wanted to find a new challenge.

I rang him up after his first inspection. He said: 'I'm not sure it's my thing, putting my head round a class-room door and seeing a young teacher's eyes fill with fear.' I have not heard, before or since, the setting described with such emotional accuracy and crispness. Almost always, the human effects of an inspection are ignored in the welter of paper.

It made me feel concerned that I had never experienced something that almost all teachers dread, neither as an inspector (God forbid!) nor as a teacher. I am of the generation that did not have to decide whether they were active fighters or conscientious objectors against Hitler. Now I was one of those who had never even had the choice about facing the might of Ofsted. I could do something about it, and when I was asked to work in a school during an inspection, I jumped at the chance.

An Ofsted Inspection (unsatisfactory)

I was told that there are five things that inspectors must do:

How to Teach with a Hangover

1 Evaluate objectively, be impartial . . .
2 Report honestly and fairly, ensuring that judgements are accurate and reliable.
3 Carry out work with integrity, treating all those they meet with courtesy and sensitivity.
4 Do all they can to minimize the stress on those involved in the inspection, and act with their best interests and well-being as priorities.
5 Maintain purposeful and productive dialogue with those being inspected, and communicate judgements clearly and frankly . . .

I was doing my day job, working with poetry and children in a school in the north of England, when I saw at first hand Ofsted raising its head over the trenches. I'd heard rumours about what an inspection was like: I had been close to an infant school where inspectors included comments on a lesson on nutrition which had happened in another school, and where, against the rules, the 'serious weaknesses' judgement had been delivered at the end of the week during which all the comments had been positive. As the four inspectors sat making notes, listening to, and sometimes actually watching lessons, I got my notebook out.

A tall woman, power-dressed in a magenta suit and clipping high heels appears suddenly in a Year 6 classroom, reminding me of a large pair of shears. I'm there, on the face of it, because I am to teach the class next.

The teacher is setting the children a task on Victorian England. The inspector's eyes move round the room, to watch children as they answer questions. She begins making notes. Then, when the children are writing, she asks the teacher something that, despite my best shameless efforts, I can't hear. The teacher shakes her head: she doesn't know the answer. Both women are slightly bothered about this. But it is clearly the teacher's, not the inspector's problem. The inspector can wait, and she does. The teacher looks worriedly through papers on her desk, hoping the right one will slip into her hand. The children write silently. A girl's hand is in the air, but the teacher is intent on finding a piece of paper.

The inspector is not really researching or evaluating this classroom at all, but (and this is a crucial difference) *the classroom is affected by her presence.*

She could, if she chose, minimize the effect she is having in two ways: by making her presence less chilly, and by keeping her questions till after the lesson. Were she to help the children, she would affect the setting, too: but in a useful way. As it is, she is like a woman who pulls the legs off a spider and tells it to walk; and when it remains still, she says 'See – pulling the legs off a spider makes it deaf'.

The inspector is still waiting for the piece of paper. The teacher is still searching. The girl's hand is still in the air. I scribble.

Later in the staffroom, all the teachers' heads turn

when anyone enters, even though the Ofsted team has its own space. This is the library, in fact, and that is another way in which the setting is distorted by their presence: during the days of the inspection, the children cannot use the books. When the staffroom door opens, and it is only the caretaker, or me, or a parent, or a teaching assistant, their shoulders drop with mini-relief. The caretaker is evidently a puzzled man. His normally easy relationship with the teachers is under strain. Someone says, 'They're in bad cop mode today, not so friendly'. The teachers evidently believe that the inspection team decides coolly each day in the car park whether to be friendly, indifferent or downright hostile.

I watch as, just outside the staffroom, a teacher flying from her classroom is captured. The inspector questions her; listens; asks another question. This may be a good way of extracting information, but it disorientates the teacher who, like a human being, is used to having her answers responded to, not ignored. Not only is the nature of the classroom changed. So is the conventional mode of human talk. The inspector never pretends that this is a conversation between equals; or even any kind of conversation. The teacher is released, and comes into the staffroom rolling her eyes.

A curiosity occurs to me, not for the first time. In the revival of traditional values that successive governments have called for – the learning of tables, arithmetic without calculators, formal numeracy and literacy lessons, competitive sport, school uniforms – two traditional values, courtesy and manners, seem to have been excluded. They are values that inspectors need not bother with. The inspector just outside the classroom had already asked me about an assembly I'd led, and then interrupted, a millisecond before the main verb of my first sentence – 'Excuse me, I must go and talk to some children'. The inspectors seem to me to be proud that they are bringing the brusque efficiency of the business workplace into the normally more humane setting of the school. What do Ofsted personnel use for contraceptives? I remember someone asking. You don't know? I'll tell you later.

I don't swear much, myself, except, of course, when vacuuming the stairs or approaching a tailback on the M25, but now I let fly with a tiny barrage of under-breath obscenities.

There is more lecturing going on in school today than would be normal. Teachers stand at whiteboards explaining things with chalk and felt tips, sentences and diagrams. They seem to assume that Ofsted would approve of this, and they may well be right. The inspection is pushing the children backwards into a passive-learner mode. Children are making fewer choices than usual, because, partly, the teachers are intent on control, both of the children and of the environment. They are keen, above all, to minimize risk, although they know, deep down, that all real learning involves at least some element of risk – risk of failure, risk of emotional involvement, risk of learning something above and beyond what the teacher is teaching. Here, today, there is little movement, little talk, little reasoning, little choice.

Something happens that infuriates me. I am taking a lesson with 8 year olds. I have just read them the speech from *A Midsummer Night's Dream* that begins 'I'll follow you' (Act 3, Scene I). It has been a serious, hilarious 5 minutes of lighting up time. I've said the words, I've got them to say them in different ways – loudly, aggressively, in a crescendo, whispering, in a Prince Charles voice – and they are just about to write their own poems with the same first line.

An inspector comes in, beckons to the teacher, and, after whispered discussions, they take four children out. Gradually, all the children's attention – 100 per cent 5 minutes ago – has evaporated as they've watched their friends leave. The reading of Shakespeare's words has petered out. The children wonder, where are they going? The little room where they test children? The firing squad? The pub? (We could all do with a drink.) What is going to happen to them? Will it be me next? I reckon my lesson has dropped from above the magic Ofsted line to below it in a few minutes; all because of Ofsted, I murmur unpleasantly to myself in silent fury.

These inspectors make no attempt to fade into the

background. They distort the school with their noise, and with the fear they cause. You wonder what this particular lack of a smile portends for you and your life – in the immediate future (humiliation) and, perhaps in the distant feature (the sack). They are everywhere. Like reverse Cheshire cats, glimpsed above the frosted glass of windows they become walking frowns drifting round corridors. I am desperate to tell the inspectors what I think about their behaviour, and if I were the head, I would do so.

The head, meanwhile, feeds back to the staff every jittery moment she or he has had with an inspector. A teacher makes to leave the staffroom with a cup of tea. 'Don't spill that on a child!' says the boss. The head said to me, as the hall where I was about to lead assembly was filling up with unusually quiet children, 'Make sure you get some spiritual and reflective stuff in'. I did. I asked the children to close their eyes and think of another child to whom they could do something kind today. The silence was intense. The head thought it was great.

I would like to know what the children made of it all. A Year 6 boy tells me, unsolicited, that when an inspector comes near his desk, 'I pretend I'm going to my tray so's they can't ask me anything'. Another child says 'I'm scared they might ask me something that I don't know . . . I don't want my teacher to get into trouble'. Another girl says 'You could say something and not know if they're listening'. That's what some of the teachers felt, I find out later.

An 8-year-old girl in another school was asked to write 'Lines to an Inspector'. She wrote:

> You asked questions, and we had to say Yes. Why did you have to ask so many questions? Besides it is an inspection, not a quiz show. You kept on nagging on and on. Why did you always look in the register? I think you were counting the days we missed school. All my life people have been saying DO NOT TALK TO STRANGERS! You're a stranger. It feels irritating when you look in our school work. And it's our privacy.

Another child wrote 'What do you do to the report? Couldn't you judge the school on SATs?' And another:

> I feel that your inspections are unnecessary because the whole school is told to be on their best behaviour and you do not see the school as it really is. I know it's for a good cause, but the way you investigate the cause seriously needs looking at.

And finally:

> I don't think inspections are necessary because it's our school and our job to make sure it's safe and everyone gets along, not yours.

Teaching with Ofsted Present

Education has always accommodated teachers who are concerned with management and checking, and not learning (their own or the children's). Measurement, rather, is everything. The last few years have driven these people to positions where they can indulge themselves, and here are two of them; one in a pink suit, another, unnaturally straight-backed, who has evidently (so the deputy heads whisper to me) had a snooker cue put to unusual and painful use. Here they are, taking the old rule to an extreme: if you can't teach, inspect.

Given all the pressure to inspect, and report fast, it is no wonder that lessons in one school drift through a computer on to another school's report; no wonder there are inconsistencies between what inspectors say and what they write; no wonder big mistakes are made which have no effect on the inspectors' lives, but which drive headteachers to despair, and turn good teachers to pale, nervy imitations of their normal professional selves.

Ofsted had bred a new generation of parasites. Advisers retire and emerge as people who will, for a consideration of a few hundred pounds, prepare your school for an Ofsted inspection. They will tell you how to adjust your management systems so that they comply with modern requirements, and how to make your curriculum documents what the government requires. These people are ex-teachers who, like the inspectors, are not concerned with children, teaching and learning, but with checklists and league tables. They quite like the look of fear on a teacher's face, and they save on birth control by using their personalities.

Since I wrote all this, there have been changes in the inspection process. There are to be fewer lesson observations, and more reliance on the schools' paperwork. Whether these changes make things better or worse remains to be seen. I suspect it will lessen the pain for teachers, and gaze with intensity on the largely irrelevant.

6 'Challenging' Children and Managing their Behaviour

My pack of unruly hounds

D. H. Lawrence

There are more ways of doing evil than the obvious ones, like violence and rape and torture and war. There's mental cruelty, and unfaithfulness, and the breaking of promises. There's telling lies, and there's telling truths 'with bad intent', which, as Blake says 'beats all the lies you can invent'.

There are ways of doing evil in schools that are less obvious than they might be. Not ways for children to be evil, or at least naughty, or, in the modern cant word, 'challenging'. Everyone knows about those: bad things in schools are conventionally seen as things children do. They not only cannot be trusted to learn, but they constantly, deliberately and maliciously frustrate teachers' efforts to teach them. That is certainly part of the myth that underpins the teachers' views of the first school that I describe below.

But most often evil is done by those in power, not by children: it is done, in descending order, by politicians, inspectors, headteachers and teachers. It's a kind of cascading model of evil: it comes from the top, and trickles down. This chapter is about those ways of doing evil, and how, as teachers, we should deal with them. Of course, as in life, the behaviour problems that children present will appear in my text. But I take it for granted that those problems pale beside problems that the institution is responsible for.

The First School

The head, who greeted me at the gate (normally a good sign), had a bad cold and shouldn't have been in school. He was there, though, greeting visitors, cornering children caught fighting and talking to parents. He was anticipating teaching, because four other teachers (among a staff of about 20) were off sick, two of them long term. No doubt he was planning lessons desperately in his head: I remember it well. A kind of undefeated pluck exuded from him.

Children and Managing their Behaviour

The building, on a sunny day, would remind you, if you are as old as I am, of a hospital of the 1950s, with green and cream corridors and metal doors hardly glazed at all, and if glazed, glazed with frosted glass. 'You shouldn't be looking in here,' they seem to say. I thought of the verrucas and appendix operations of my childhood. I don't mean a hospital of today, with attempts to brighten the environment and to surround the patients, doctors and nurses with art (Poppies in a Field Near Aldeburgh; Fishing Boats Drawn up on the Beach at Southwold), a café near the front entrance serving cappuccinos and croissants and a paper shop with the full range of newspapers and magazines. This school is like the sort of hospital that used to make you feel guilty for being ill.

On gloomy days, and today is a gloomy day, with leaden January skies, and rain spitting on the windscreen as I pull the car into the car park, this school reminds you of a prison. As I swap small talk with the head, it is noisy, in a way that is incipient with aggression, with the clashing of doors and children's shouts. Inside, it is worse, because the acoustics exacerbate the noise. The school has never, apparently, fallen among Plowdenite teachers with a passion for art and display. The display boards are covered with posters and notices exhorting the children to read, not to drop litter, not to talk to strangers and not to run. One poster asks, plaintively, which class will win the most headteacher's stickers this week. Most of them have been there a long time.

In the staffroom two teachers drink cheap instant coffee from a catering tin with UHT milk. These are two surefire signs of a school on its emotional and professional uppers – no one can be bothered to buy decent coffee or collect fresh milk. They complained of the image they were presenting. 'Sorry, but we're a bit stretched today . . .' The grumbles, as usual, concerned government policies, the local authority's advisers and the increasing administrative workload. But mostly, and this is unusual, it concerned the children. 'The behaviour of these kids is just something I want to walk away from . . . that was why the last head left, she couldn't stand the constant confrontation . . .' The teachers off long term, I was told, were suffering from stress.

Later I saw the present head leaning over a boy: 'Why did you kick Marie? Say sorry now, and mean it.' Grudgingly, the boy complied. A 'sorry' demanded is the most meaningless word I know.

During the day, it emerged that the teachers had a myth about the school and its problems. By 'myth', I mean a narrative that tries to explain elements of our predicament to ourselves, much as the myth of the fall in Genesis tries to explain our wicked actions as human beings, or the myth of the Tower of Babel offers an attempt at understanding the multiplicity of human languages and the dangers of human pride. It was central to the teachers' myth that the local units for dis-ruptive children had been closed down, and that those children were all here now. And that was making life unbearable.

Indeed, one boy in a class I taught had very little idea about what to do with the writing idea I'd given him. All those others were scribbling away, many of them with great passion – for the moment they wanted to be poets when they grew up – but this boy forced out his effort letter by letter, rather than word by word, or sentence by sentence. He was adrift both from the words he was trying to write, and from his classmates, and would have been, only a few years ago, in an area special class. A learning support assistant sat with him, painstakingly sounding out the words he spoke so that he could write them down. At playtime, he showed all the signs of his alienation. Solitary one minute, the next he would be interfering with a game, or taunting a group of girls.

So I don't dispute that there is some literal truth in this myth, this idea that the school was being held back, and the teachers challenged, by children who should have been receiving special care. There is some literal truth in most, though not all, myths. I felt sorry for those teachers, and grateful that I was hit-and-run, and would be away up the M4 by 3.15pm. By myth I mean a story that helps us to understand, however partially, what we are going through. I might have had a different myth about this school, concerned, perhaps, with the clanging doors, the lack of grass and art, the morale-sapping league tables that only a month before had been published, placing this school in the bottom twenty-odd primary schools in the county.

Teachers need to examine their myth when they complain of bad behaviour. It had become all-pervading here, and I believe it hid other more hopeful truths about their school. The teachers simply didn't see the many children, by far the majority, who wrote well, who were committed to making their poems, who were behaving well, who played together amicably on the playground. The slow boy, the boy on the yard who had been fighting, these boys became for those teachers the whole reality. They became the myth by which the teachers defined their school.

And then they need to examine their own behaviour, and the behaviour of everyone with power over the children. I felt that the teachers in this school were kind, but that institutional bullying exerted a baleful pressure. I thought of children who are treated badly and how as they grow up a vicious cycle repeats itself. I tried to make this point in a poem (Sedgwick 1986):

The Ballad of Darren Cullen

This is the case of Darren Cullen
   (Blue eyes, six foot three)
His Dad, his teacher (Mrs Spence)
   And his headmaster (me).

Children and Managing their Behaviour

Big Darren's Daddy picked him up
    When the lad was two foot tall
And swung him by the ankles hard
    Against the bedroom wall.

Young Darren leaned around the back
    Of the Star and Garter Inn
While his Daddy bought his Auntie Chris
    Her seventh double gin.

And when the boy was five foot tall
    They caught him in Grigson's Yard
Driving a forklift truck around
    The piles of packing card.

Down by the condomy canal
    In Calvinistic weather
Darren reached the start of his youth
    And the end of his short tether.

His teacher, knowing the school was built
    For her own peace and quiet,
Gently tickled in him one day
    His tendency to riot.

'Nobody loves you Darren Cullen
    And I will tell you why . . .'
She said, and found no going on
    For the death in Darren's eye.

How to Teach with a Hangover

He's taken from a new display
    Of farming implements
A horse mane docker, and it's aimed
    At Mrs Muriel Spence.

Oh bloody hell the headmaster thinks
    And his lunge is rather tardy –
The thing is sticking neatly out
    From Mrs Spence's cardy.

After a vivid afternoon
    They found out what you've guessed:
The horse mane docker hardly got
    Beyond Mu Spence's vest.

Thank God, we said. Darren was carted
    Off to special school
For scaring a teacher witless with
    An agricultural tool.

These days the lad is six foot three
    And he takes his revenge on all
His women nightly, and the little lad
    That he bangs on the bedroom wall.

There are many kinds of determinism, notably religious (Calvinist), political (Marxist) and behaviourist (Skinnerite), and I believe in none of them. I believe in our ability as human beings (in Dylan Thomas's lovely phrase from 'Fern Hill') to 'sing in [our] chains like the sea'. But it is also true that violence on the young will breed more violence. And the act, in which we are all, to some extent or other, complicit, of imprisoning children in a jail made of SATs, league tables and the rest, will one day generate its own evil.

We can do nothing about the wrongs done to children before we meet them, when they are in the womb (malnutrition, smoking, drinking), in the cradle, in their infancy (neglect, torture) or in their diet (Big Macs and Sunny Delight). We can do nothing about damage done to them by the environment (the media, pollution, the state of their school, the state of the streets where they live). We can do nothing about what nature has done to them: an autistic child presents his or her problems to us because of factors beyond our control and usually beyond our ken.

But we can influence the children. We can soften some of the effects of a harsh environment, and we can provide another environment, the school, that offers an unsentimental love. We can suffer the children to come: of such is the Kingdom of Heaven.

The Second School

Here is another school, this time in the north of England. It lies among depressed back-to-back housing, and in the near distance there is a state-of-the-art football stadium. This stadium means that everyone in the neighbourhood is faced with its riches and glamour, and memories of the meaningless grandiosity of sporting success as they walk around their dingy streets. Like television advertisements at Christmas, it is a constant reproach to poverty and failure, like the Jaguar garage in my own town that, at night, is in the centre of the red-light district.

You might easily stereotype the children here as being difficult. They evidently aren't well fed. They have that pale, drawn look of children who are always close to hunger. They don't have gardens. But they aren't difficult. The teachers' myth about this school, promulgated initially, I suspect, by the cheerful headteacher, is that the children here are as good as any children in the country, and that they deserve the best we can give them. And by heaven, we are going to give it to them. What had the teachers done to fulfil this myth?

First, they had changed the environment. Hospitals have changed because of an understanding that what is around us affects our welfare almost as much as what people do for us. In the school, the walls belonged to the children. They were covered with their paintings and poems, and the displays had been in part arranged by them. These displays were not part of an ego trip by a teacher, or an attempt to sell the school to the next inspector to call. Most important of all, they weren't sterile posters, unnoticed by anybody a day after they were pinned up.

Second, the teachers' attitudes towards the children were unremittingly positive. Not, I must say, in the dubious modern way of praising absolutely everything ('I love the way you have written that "T", John'; 'I must say thank you to Year 2 for coming into assembly so quietly').

The teachers simply expected the children to do well, so they did. I once saw a display of ceramics in the entrance hall of a school. 'Aren't you afraid of the pots getting broken?' I asked the head. 'Things only get broken in schools where it is expected,' she replied. By the same token, if we expect children to write well, they will. We can express that confidence in many ways: a cheerful optimism that comes from success in the past, a simple statement of what the children are going to do, a genuine respect for the children however they present to us. It is more difficult to expect the children not to break the pottery in the entrance hall. That comes from a trusting stance to life, from a belief that the light of God shines in every human being.

Third, they have taken the notion of respect and turned it on its head. It is conventional for schools to demand respect from the children. But does the school, and the behaviour of its adults, show respect for the children? There are so many ways of showing disrespect, and some of them are ways that I thought had disappeared in the 1970s. I was wrong. Here, for example, is a notice in a classroom in the first school. It says: How many stars have you got this term? And here are the children's names, in alphabetical order:

Amy [here are 12 stamps, each saying 'Well Done']

Amrit 15

Chloe 12

Daisy 2

Freddie 5

Do I need to continue? From the publication of this data on the classroom wall, Amy, Amrit, Chloe, Daisy and Freddie can all deduce with no trouble at all how much they are respected by their teacher. And Daisy and Freddie are expected to respect their teacher?

Not Assertive Discipline

In my nephew's last year at primary school, the regime (and I use the word advisedly, with its suggestion of dodgy governments in countries we think are inferior to ours) introduced a disciplinary system. It can be summed up in the notices that appeared in every classroom.

Children and Managing their Behaviour

First offence: Name written on the blackboard. Reprimand from the teacher.

Second offence: Sent to Mr Canterbury [deputy head].

Third offence: Sent to Mrs Tompkins [headteacher].

Fourth offence: Phone call to parents.

Fifth offence: Meeting with parents and head-teacher.

My nephew played the school game well. This does not mean that he was an especially good boy, though he may have been that. It means that he knew how to walk away from trouble. In fact, it emerged later during his secondary years, that many of the bad lads (this is not sexist language, it is the truth) had been among his best friends. But he hated the names on blackboards, and the way it encouraged other children to act like coppers' narks. He hated the clinical collecting of penalty points, as if the children were speeding motorists, or ill-disciplined footballers. Assertive discipline seems to mean zero tolerance, and, as a result, a concentration on even the most trivial of offences, and an atmosphere of constant confrontation.

A Word About Special Needs

I have always felt that this term was an honourable attempt in 1978 to reform the thinking behind terms like 'retarded', 'backward', and 'remedial'. All those dreadful old words had been used to imprison children in terms of their performances in tests of varying sophistication. Most of those tests were biased against children both ethnically and in terms of social class. The terms are inhumane words. I know something of their effect personally: I was in remedial maths in my grammar school in south London many years ago, until they invented a fourth set. Then I was relegated. I didn't feel good about that.

'Special needs' seems to be a healthier term, of course, because it implies inclusion and integration rather than separation. It was also part of a move to make sure children seen in this way still had (another vogue word of the 1970s coming up) entitlement to the main curriculum. They were not to be locked into phonetic and arithmetical training. But it hasn't improved things much. Teachers used to label children with the old vile terms, and now they label them with 'special needs'.

Tyrrell Burgess (2002) has no time for it. It is, for him, 'a mealy-mouthed phrase disguising a shift of blame for educational failure from schools and public authorities to children'. This is so unfashionable, so negative, that it deserves some analysis. The children that I see failing are almost all taught in unpleasant settings, like the school I have described above. Almost always, the teachers have become accustomed to expecting little from these children, and therefore they offer them less than they should. And when you look at the names of schools at the bottom of any authority's league tables, you can see at once that the unpleasantness of these settings extends way beyond the school walls, on to (quite often) the lack of any grass; and out into the most depressing, deprived areas in the country, where work is scarce and malnutrition incipient if not actually present. In my authority, St Mary's Church of England in Leafy Village always comes top, and Dead End Primary, on the Concrete Estate, always comes last. The failings are not in the children. They are not even mainly in the schools. They are in the society that perpetrates injustice.

But as we have to live with the settings we work in, and with the phrase, I will start by saying that all children have special needs, not just the children so labelled. The point is best made by saying that all adults have special needs, too. Now I don't want to minimize the needs of people confined to wheelchairs, or who have mental diseases. I know that their needs are greater than those of nearly all of us. But understanding that we all have special needs is likely to help us to understand that to be human is to be in need at some time or another, or, in many cases, all the time.

How to Teach with a Hangover

It is also likely to help us to understand that the person we see with the obvious special need, symbolized by that wheelchair, has an expertise denied to us, whether it is Wittgenstein's philosophy, country and western music, gardening, the Buddhist religion or the wives of Henry VIII. But, unfortunately, many of us take the wheelchair for an all-encompassing statement, and define them by it. Who cares about what they know about the Tractatus, Nashville, their loved herb garden, the Buddha or Anne Boleyn?

My friend Norma is something of an expert on English and Irish literature, especially James Joyce's novel *Ulysses*. She also knows more than anyone else I know about sign language. But she is a poor speller. She has a respectable job in the Health Service, but she feels that her partner must check every report she writes. Is this trivial? It seemed to me to be so until one day I casually corrected a spelling mistake she'd made, and her cheeks reddened, and she told me a story of real or imagined humiliations.

With children, there are the obvious special needs. A boy had difficulty in reading from his nursery days until he left for secondary school. What happened then, I don't know. But one afternoon, on a walk, I encountered him with his older brothers beside the reservoir. What he knew about fishing – the bait, the gear, the fish themselves – represented, probably, a larger proportion of what I am going to call the fishing knowledge than I

have about the poetry knowledge. And I have been reading and studying and writing about poetry for more
than 45 years. Labelled 'special needs' in school, he
didn't deserve that label in one important area of his life
and quite likely in others, too. But were his teachers ever
going to find out about that? Did they care?

Danny was my son's contemporary at school, and
failed at nearly everything. Literacy and numeracy were
words that stood for things forbidding and alien. But
(my son tells me now) watch him strip a motorbike
engine and put it back together again with an efficiency
which neither my son nor (saving some miracle) I will
ever match. He knew the meanings of words that will
always be a mystery to us: carburettor, oil filter, spark
plugs.

Gifted children are sometimes seen as having no special needs. But in many schools they do have problems.
Sometimes, their intellect is bigger than the teacher's,
and they don't get the stimulation they need, especially
if the teacher is unable to direct them towards books,
other teachers or Internet sites.

Or perhaps they are incapacitated by their own clev-
erness. One professor of mathematics told me a story
from his childhood. When he was 5 years old, he
impressed his parents, aunts and uncles (one of whom
was a leading authority on genetics) with his advanced
mathematical knowledge. Everyone, mostly senior aca-
demics with PhDs and books to their names, clapped,

glad and proud, I suppose, that he was to travel in their footsteps.

He was sent to bed, but reappeared in tears and pyjamas. I imagine those pyjamas now, flannelled, no doubt, striped, probably, wrongly buttoned, almost certainly. He was crying because he couldn't get the top off the toothpaste.

Special needs? What, reader, is your problem? You have a temper that throws life off balance every so often? You are so shy that talk at dinner parties brings you out in a sweat? You can't change a tyre? I am embarrassed by my failure to learn to swim. Well, thank God, none of us is perfect. And being sure of that helps us to be more tolerant of, and gain a greater understanding of, those children in our schools who are clamped down with a label.

'Don't expect much from her, she's special needs,' I am often told, with a surreptitious finger pointing out a child. Sometimes the finger is not so surreptitious. One teacher put her arm round a boy's shoulders, and told me, 'Johnny has trouble with writing, but he's done well today'. But watch those children after school, riding a horse, or fishing, dancing in a ballet class or singing in a rock band. And listen to their talk about these subjects. If we get these children to write about their obsessions, rather than some dreary topic provided by the National Curriculum, they won't be special needs, at least for the time being.

Children and Managing their Behaviour

Children – all children, as the teachers of Reggio Emilia say – come to us with 100 languages, and we try to take them all away, except our school language.

Who's special needs? We all are. And the biggest special needs are in the system that labels children with that well-meaning but essentially inhumane tag. Label a child, insult him. Put her down. Humiliate him. Somebody, somewhere, will pay the price, because if we hurt someone, they will go on to hurt us, or someone else.

References

Amis, Kingsley (1972) *On Drink*, London: Cape.

Auden, W. H. (1976) *Collected Poems*, edited by E. Mendelson, London: Faber.

Barker, Juliet (1994) *The Brontës*, London: Weidenfeld and Nicholson.

Bennett, Alan (1968) *Forty Years On*, London: Faber and Faber.

Blake, William (1958) *A Selection of Poems and Letters*, edited with an Introduction by J. Bronowsky, London: Penguin.

Burgess, Tyrrell (2002) *The Devil's Dictionary of Education*, London: Continuum.

Causley, Charles (1992) *Collected Poems*, London: Macmillan.

Dickens, Charles (all Penguin Classics) *David Copperfield, Nicholas Nickleby, Hard Times*.

References

Eliot, T. S. (1969) *The Complete Poems and Plays*, London: Faber and Faber.

Harris, John (15 January 2005) 'What a Creation' in the *Guardian Weekend*.

John, Jeffrey (1993) *Permanent, Faithful, Stable*, London: Dartman, Longman and Todd.

Joyce, James (1916, 1992) *Portrait of the Artist as a Young Man*, New York: Barnes and Noble.

—— *Ulysses* (1912, 1992), London: Everyman.

Lang, Peter (ed.) (1988) *Thinking about Personal and Social Education in the Primary School*, Oxford: Basil Blackwell.

Larkin, Philip (1988) *Collected Poems*, edited by A. Thwaite, London: Faber.

Lawrence, D. H. (1994) *The Works of D H Lawrence*, London: Wordsworth Poetry Library.

Milton, John (1872) *The Poetical Works of John Milton*, London: Frederick Warne.

Morgan, Edwin (1990) *Collected Poems*, Manchester: Carcarnet.

Orwell, George (1961) *Collected Essays*, London: Heinemann.

Powell, Anthony (1977) *A Dance to the Music of Time*, London: Mandarin.

Pullman, Philip (22 January 2005) 'Common sense has much to learn from moonshine' in the *Guardian*.

Rae, Simon (ed.) (1991) *The Faber Book of Drink, Drinkers and Drinking*, London: Faber and Faber.

Rosen, Michael (1994) *The Penguin Book of Childhood*, London: Viking.

Sedgwick, Fred (10 August 1987) 'In at the naff end' in *The Times Educational Supplement*.

—— *The Living Daylights* (1986), Liverpool: Headland.

—— *Shakespeare and the Young Writer* (1999), London: Routledge.

—— *Enabling Children's Learning Through Drawing* (2002), London: David Fulton.

Sendak, Maurice (1963) *Where the Wild Things Are*, New York: HarperCollins.

Shakespeare, William (1966) *Love's Labour's Lost*, edited by R. David, London: Routledge.

—— *A Midsummer Night's Dream* (1984) edited by L. Buckle and P. Kelley, Cambridge: Cambridge University Press.

Smithers, Rebecca (4 February 2005) 'Woodhead over-rode inspectors to fail improving school' in the *Guardian*.

Whitehead, Frank (1966) *The Disappearing Dais: A study of the principles and practice of English teaching*, London: Chatto and Windus.

Wragg, Ted (7 September 2004) 'So "creative teaching" is the new government idea? . . .' in the *Guardian*.

Thomas, Dylan (1952) *Collected Poems 1934–1952*, London: Dent.

Vengler, Helen (1998) *Seamus Heaney*, London: Harper and Collins.

References

Wells, Gordon (1986) *The Meaning Makers: Children Learning Language and Using Language to Learn*, London: Hodder & Stoughton.

White, John (1990) *Education and the Good Life: Beyond the National Curriculum*, London: Kogan Page.

Whitehead, Frank (1966) *The Disappearing Dais*, London: Chatto and Windus.